STRANGE BUT TRUE

Strange Vanishings

STRANGE BUT TRUE

Strange Vanishings

COLIN WILSON

Sterling Publishing Co., Inc.
New York

Library of Congress
Cataloging-in-Publication Data Available

10 9 8 7 6 5 4 3 2 1

Published in the United States and Canada in 1997 by
Sterling Publishing Company, Inc
387 Park Avenue South, New York, NY 10016–8810

Originally published in Great Britain in 1997. Produced by Magpie Books,
an imprint of Robinson Publishing Ltd.

Copyright © Robinson Publishing Ltd, 1997

Illustrations courtesy of Popperfoto

Distributed in Canada by Sterling Publishing
c/o Canadian Manda Group, One Atlantic Avenue, Suite 105
Toronto, Ontario, Canada M6K 3E7

ISBN 0–8069–0585–9

Printed and bound in the E.C.

Contents

1

Vanishings and Reappearances

One evening in 1939, a normal American family – mother, father, two teenage brothers and a sister – were sitting around a table eating a holiday dinner. The father, who was a musician and a teacher, was looking a little tired and absent-minded. Suddenly, in the middle of the dinner, he pushed back his chair and said, "I'm going to get a pack of cigarettes."

His family looked at him in astonishment – he didn't smoke. But no one raised any objection as he walked out of the house, got into his car, and drove away.

That was the last time anyone in his family saw him. His car was found parked outside the grocery store in the nearby town. But no one had seen him. Eight or nine years later, he was declared legally dead.

It sounds a commonplace enough story. An overworked music teacher walks out on his family, and disappears – perhaps to go and live on the other side of the country with a mistress. What is so unusual about that?

What was unusual would begin to emerge more than half a century later, at a conference that took place at the Massachusetts Institute of Technology in June 1992. The subject of the conference was alien abductions – people who were firmly convinced that they had been abducted by the occupants of UFOs – or flying saucers – and had subsequently suffered a kind of amnesia about their experiences.

Alien Experiences

The new wave of interest in UFO abductions had started in 1981, with the publication of a book called *Missing Time*, by New York artist Budd Hopkins. One evening, six years earlier, Hopkins had walked into his local liquor store and found its owner, 72-year-old George O'Barski looking shaken and worried. He told Hopkins, "A man can be driving home, minding his own business, and something can come down out of the sky and scare you half to death."

Now Hopkins happened to be interested in the subject of Flying Saucers, and he hurried off home to get a tape recorder. When he returned, the liquor store owner told him how, one evening, he had been driving home towards New Jersey when a brilliantly lit object passed overhead, travelling in the same direction. Then he saw it land in a nearby field, near a block of flats. To George's amazement, a door opened in the side of the craft, which was circular and about thirty feet across, and a number of strange figures emerged. They were about three and a half feet tall, dressed in identical helmets or hoods, and one piece garments. "They looked like kids in snow-suits."

George O'Barski's story led Budd Hopkins on a quest that involved interviews with dozens of people who found that fragments of their lives seemed to be missing – sometimes a few hours, sometimes even days.

That is why hundreds of people converged on the Massachusetts Institute of Technology at Cambridge,

Massachusetts on June 13, 1992. And among those crowds there were two women who ran a horse farm in Maryland. Hopkins concealed their identities under the names Carol Dedham and Alice Bartlett.

Alien Abduction

These two had had a whole series of abduction experiences, which they described at the conference. And later, they published their own story of these abductions in a book called *Connections: Solving Our Alien Abduction Mystery*. This time, they give their names as Beth Collings and Anna Jamerson. Beth Collings was the granddaughter of the man who disappeared from the dinner table in 1939 and vanished.

In retrospect, and in the light of the book *Connections*, it begins to look more and more probable that Carol's grandfather was an earlier example of UFO abduction. And, moreover, that Carol's father had gone through the same experience.

To those who feel that all this sounds slightly insane, and certainly too absurd to be taken seriously, I would recommend a book called *Close Encounters of the Fourth Kind*, by C. D. B. Bryan, which is a lengthy account of that five day conference at the Massachusetts Institute of Technology. It leaves no doubt whatever that the subject of alien abduction is something that we ought to be taking very seriously indeed. For, as Courty Bryan says in his introduction,

One might reasonably expect that a 'scientific conference' on such a subject as people who have reported

3

their abduction by 'little green men' ought to be dismissed out of hand and it certainly would have been but for the credentials of those chairing it, the site of the conference . . . . and the disturbing credibility, generally speaking, of the hundreds of individuals who, uncontaminated by exposure to any previous unidentified flying object lore or to each other, have so hesitantly, reluctantly, *timidly* come forward with their utterly incredible accounts of having being abducted and examined in UFOs not by 'little green men' but rather, for the most part, by spindly-limbed, 3.5 to 4.5 foot tall telepathic gray creatures with outsized foreheads dominated by huge, compelling, tear-shaped black eyes. And it is in the similarities of these abductees' stories and the consistency of their details that the true mystery lies. For as John Mack would ask at the Abduction Study Conference, 'If what these abductees are saying is happening to them *isn't* happening, what is?' For it is no longer a question of a dozen or so more people spread across a continent who are claiming these weird experiences. It is literally *thousands* of people all over the world.

So let me, before we go any further, offer a little background material.

Missing Time

As far as I can ascertain, the first report of "missing time" occurred as far back as 1953. The scene was Tujunga Canyon, California. Two young women, whose identities were concealed under the names Sarah Shaw and Jan Whitley were engaged in a lesbian relationship, and were living together in the Tujunga Canyons between Los Angeles and the Mojave desert.

The two women were asleep on the night of March 22, 1953, when Sarah was awakened by a bright light which swept across the wall, giving the impression of a car or a motor cycle driving past. For a moment, she thought that a motor cycle gang who had caused damage earlier might have returned, and shook Jan awake. The time she saw was exactly 2 a.m. She knelt on the bed to look out of the window, and suddenly felt giddy and confused. At this point she glanced at the clock again, and realised that the time was already 4.20 a.m. Two hours had gone past. The two women were so upset that they left the cabin and did not return for several days.

In 1975, the two decided to submit to hypnosis in an attempt to find out what had happened during those two hours and twenty minutes. Now, Sarah remembered that she and Jan had been taken out of their cabin and floated up onto a UFO, which was hovering in the sky above. There they were undressed, examined by machines and then by aliens who wore black body-stockings and communicated telepathically with them (including a cure for cancer), and finally floated back to the cabin. Sarah said that she enjoyed the attention of the male aliens while she was lying naked. Jan, on the other hand, was unable to recall anything of what had happened during the period of missing time.

Psychic investigator Scott Rogo, who interviewed the women, decided that the whole thing was simply a fantasy, and that Sarah was expressing her dissatisfaction with her lesbian relationship. He points out that Sarah later entered a normal marriage. But if Rogo were

On the morning of October 25, 1593, people in the main square (Plaza Mayor) in Mexico City were startled by the sudden appearance of a soldier who seemed to have come from nowhere. He was wearing the uniform of a regiment which at that moment was in Manila (in the Philippines), 9,000 miles away. He seemed bewildered and asked where he was. When told that he was in Mexico City, he refused to believe it. Later, questioned by the authorities, he explained that he had been in Manila, when quite suddenly he had found himself in Mexico City.

Assuming he was a deserter, the authorities threw him into prison. During his interrogation, he told them that the Governor of the Philippines, Don Gomez Perez Dasmarinas, had been murdered. He was still in prison several weeks later when news came from a ship that had docked at Acapulco – the governor indeed was dead, murdered by a mutinous Chinese crew off Punta de Azufre, just as he was setting off on a military expedition against the Molucca Islands. That had happened on the day the soldier had appeared in Mexico City.

The Inquisition, suspecting witchcraft, ordered the soldier to be returned to Manila. There, a number of witnesses declared that he had been there on duty on the night of October 24, 1593, and had then disappeared.

Don Luis Gonzales Obregon, who recounts the story in *Las Calles de Mejico*, does not mention what became of the soldier. Neither does Dr Antonio de Morga, Justice of the Criminal Court of New Spain, in his *Sucesos de las Islas Filipinas*.

alive today – he was murdered in the late 1980s in the course of a robbery – he would certainly recognize the similarity of hundreds of accounts of "missing time" and the experience of Jan and Sarah.

Eight years later, a couple named Barney and Betty Hill were involved in what has become the most famous of the early abduction cases. They were a mixed-race couple who had met through their support for civil rights. Barney was a mail sorter, while Betty was a social worker. Both were also committed Christians, and were on their churches' United Nations Committee.

In mid-September 1961, they were returning from a short holiday in Canada and were driving through the night. At nine in the evening, they had dinner then continued their drive south. When Betty noticed a bright light that seemed to be going parallel to their course along US Highway 3, Barney suggested that it might be a satellite that had gone off course. Finally, they stopped the car to look at it through binoculars, and Barney decided it was an aircraft. Finally it had come so close that Betty was able to see, through binoculars, that it was a huge craft with a double row of windows. They stopped the car, and Barney walked towards the light, which was now on the level of the trees. He was later to say that he saw an object "like a big pancake" with rows of windows and at least half a dozen occupants looking out at them. They seemed to be dressed in Nazi-style uniforms. Suddenly, Barney decided to run back to the car. As they drove away at top speed, the couple heard two sets of beeping sounds.

They reached Portsmouth after dawn, and only then realised that the drive had taken them far too long –

seven hours to cover the last 190 miles, which should have taken, at most, four hours. When they woke up again, Betty approached their car with a compass to see whether it might have picked up any kind of electro-magnetic radiation, and was surprised to find on the lid of the boot a dozen or more shiny circles. The compass showed a strong reaction when brought close to it.

Barney was inclined to forget the whole thing, but Betty insisted on ringing Pease Air Force Base and reporting the experience. The officer she spoke to told her that he had received a number of other reports about flying objects in the area.

It was after reading a book called *The Flying Saucer Conspiracy*, by Major Donald Keyhoe, alleging that the Air Force was involved in a deliberate cover-up of Flying Saucer information, that Betty decided to write the author a letter. As a result, they were visited by Walter Webb, a lecturer on the staff of the Hayden Planetarium in Boston. Webb, who had expected to find the whole thing a waste of time, became increasingly convinced as he listened to their story over several hours. He subsequently told his National Investigations Committee that he was totally convinced they were genuine. It was only when they were repeating their story yet again that the Hills suddenly recognised clearly that they had lost several hours – it was something that had not clearly struck them at the time. Someone on the Committee suggested that it might be worthwhile placing the Hills under hypnosis to see whether they could remember what had happened. They were at first unwilling, but after many attempts to remember about the "missing time" – and becoming increasingly fru-strated with the amnesia that seemed to descend upon them after recalling a beeping noise after they stopped the car – they finally decided to consult a well-known Boston psychiatrist, Dr Benjamin Simon.

Under hypnosis, Barney remembered that, after the beeps, their path had been blocked by a group of humanoids with large eyes, no nose and slitty lipless mouths. They were both taken on board the spacecraft and made to lie down on operating tables. Betty had to remove her dress, and a large needle was inserted into her navel – one of the humanoids, speaking English, told her he was testing her for pregnancy. The aliens asked many questions about what they ate and drank, and were intrigued by the fact that Barney's teeth came out. Finally, they were taken back to their car and the spacecraft took off. More beeping sounds made them aware that they were now driving away at top speed.

Although Betty and Barney told the same basic story – with certain differences – the hypnotist was inclined to believe that they were suffering from some kind of hallucination, probably induced by their fear after seeing some unknown flying object. But journalist John Fuller found their story sufficiently convincing to write a full-length book called *The Interrupted Journey* (1966), which had the effect of making the couple famous. Barney was to die three years later of a cerebral haemorrhage.

Among those who believed that Barney and Betty Hill recounted an imaginary story under hypnosis was Budd Hopkins, the man who (in the 1980s) was to make everyone aware that UFO abductions are far more commonplace than we had supposed. During the course of that decade and the early '90s, he would study more than 1,500 cases. As a result of his first book, *Missing Time*, Budd Hopkins was deluged with phone-calls from people who claimed they had had abduction experiences. Hopkins was forced to try to find helpers. And by 1990, there were UFO Research groups in most of the major states of America.

Connections

It was early in 1992 that Anna Jamerson, the co-author of *Connections*, found the phone number of one of these groups in the Washington phone book and rang them. It was this phone call that started the chain of events that led "Carol and Alice" – or Beth and Anna – to present their stories at that conference at the Massachusetts Institute of Technology – one of America's most respected scientific institutions – in June 1992.

Beth Collings, the reader will recall, was the woman whose grandfather had walked out of the house in 1939 and never returned. This, briefly, is the story she told when she stood up, shaking with nervousness, on the second day of the conference.

In 1954, when she was five-years-old, she went on a car trip with her father to Doylestown, Pennsylvania, for a meeting. It was a hot day, and they were on a dirt road between empty fields when the car suddenly stopped. Her father tried to start it, then went around and raised the bonnet to look at the engine. Beth, for some reason, was feeling terribly nervous and wanted him to come back. Quite suddenly, Beth says, the car was full of freezing air – whereas a few seconds before it had been uncomfortably hot. She began shouting for her father to return. He said some comforting words and put his arm around her shoulder. And as he was talking to her, the car suddenly started – although he had not touched the ignition key. Yet her father seemed quite unsurprised. When they reached the office building where the father was supposed to have attended a business meeting, it was already night time, and a note on the door said "Sorry I missed you." Her father then looked at his watch and said, "What's happened to the time? I had no idea it took so long!" It was after nine in the evening, and yet the place where the car had stalled was only a short drive away.

In 1987, Anna Jamerson was running a horse farm in Maryland and urgently needed some help. She advertised for a stable manager, and one Saturday afternoon, Beth Collings drove up to apply for the job. Oddly enough, Anna had a feeling that she had met her before. (A long time later they were to realise that they actually *had* met as children – meeting by complete chance and having a long conversation.) Beth loved horses as much as Anna, and during the next five years they became close friends as well as employer and employee.

The strange events began two years later in 1989. One evening, as they were watching TV, Anna's sister Nancy called them out on to the back porch and pointed at three bright lights travelling together in a triangular formation. At first, they thought they were probably the three lights of a jet airliner travelling towards them. But it seemed too low and they could hear no sound at all. Then, suddenly, the lights halted in the air above them and remained stationary. Suddenly, one of the lights broke away from the others and moved away at considerable speed, startling all three of them. It travelled for a while, stopped abruptly, and then moved away until it disappeared. Soon after that, the other two lights simply vanished as if they had been switched off.

Oddly enough, the three women disagreed about what they had seen. Nancy and Anna thought that there had been five lights, and Nancy denied flatly that she had gone off to look around at the front of the house at one point to see if there were any lights hovering there.

Things became alarming two years later, on December 15, 1991. Beth had spent the day with her parents and was driving back through the dark. Suddenly she saw three bright white lights over the top of the trees. She thought they were the same lights that she had seen with Alice and Nancy. She stopped the car and tried to get a closer look. Suddenly one of the lights moved towards her and halted directly overhead, so close that she felt she could reach up and touch it. She thought she could see blue lights on either side of the craft, and the glow was so brilliant that it hurt her eyes. She looked away to see if the other two lights were still there – and then, quite suddenly, found herself driving five miles away at tremendous speed, going around a bend so fast that the car was balancing on two wheels. When she got back to the farm, she realised that it was far later than she thought – 10.15 p.m. – when her guess was that it was about 8.30 p.m. She had seen the lights hovering overhead at 8.15 p.m.

Shortly after, in January, she was driving back to the farm with a large box of Christmas gifts containing biscuits and sweets. Once again, she saw the three bright lights overhead and groaned aloud, "Oh no!

not again!" She blinked, and then suddenly found that she was eight miles further on and that she had actually passed the farm. The contents of her briefcase were scattered in the car, and it was obvious that the Christmas package had been unwrapped and resealed with masking tape in a crude and clumsy manner. Some of the contents of the box had been removed.

Later, she talked to her father about the experience when she was a five-year-old child and he told her about her grandfather – how he had walked out of the house and vanished. Not long after that, she was sitting with her four-year-old granddaughter when she realised that the child was drawing a "flying machine" with a red light in the middle and faces looking out of the windows. Down in the corner, there was a small red figure, which her granddaughter explained was a man called Nu, who had taken her through a long tunnel that was lighted in red and had a long green stripe on the ceiling.

That night, as Beth was putting her granddaughter to bed, the child told her that Nu was "gray all over" and had big eyes and wore a flat hat. He said goodnight to her every night. And suddenly the little girl turned to the bedroom door and called "goodnight, Nu!" The open doorway was empty. But the child said "Nu is saying goodnight to you too, Grandma."

So it began to look as if contact with the UFO inhabitants who were "gray all over" had lasted over several generations.

Other people at that MIT conference had similar stories to tell. And their stories were amazingly similar. It was as if a group of people had got together to deliberately concoct tales about being taken out of their bedrooms by strange creatures with slitty eyes, physically examined inside spacecraft, and then returned with "missing time" – or temporary amnesia. Yet the astonishing thing was that the people at the conference came from all over America, and had had no opportunity to get together to concoct a story. Neither were most of them familiar with any abduction experiences except their own. And Courty Bryan, who had gone to the conference with the certainty that the whole thing would turn out to be a waste of time, became increasingly convinced that *something* was going on.

It might, of course, have been simply some strange new psychological phenomenon, some kind of mass hallucination. But the more he heard from the people present, the less he felt like accepting this simplistic explanation.

UFOs

As we shall see, there are many cases in this book which suggest that abduction by "aliens" is the obvious answer. Yet many of these took place long before the word "flying saucer" was coined. On June 24, 1947, businessman Kenneth Arnold was flying his own private aeroplane near Mount Rainier, Washington State, he saw "a formation of nine very bright objects coming from the vicinity of Mount Baker, flying very close to the mountain tops and travelling at a tremendous speed." Arnold said that, in spite of their speed, they seemed to be moving with a strange swaying motion, tipping from side to side, and emitting a very bright blue light from their surfaces. Later, Arnold described them to pressmen as "flying saucers" – saying that the objects moved "like a saucer would if you skipped it across water." It was after the Arnold sighting that thousands more reports of flying saucers began to flood in.

But in fact, there are many reports of strange flying objects that date back long before 1947. One of the most authentic can be found in a book called *Altai-Himalaya* (published in 1930), in which the painter Nicholas Roerich mentions how, on August 5, 1926, he observed a big shiny disc moving at great speed across the sky and then, quite abruptly, turning at right angles – a feat that should be impossible according to the laws of physics. Other reports of strange circular-shaped objects flying through the sky date back to the nineteenth century.

On July 24, 1924, two British pilots, Flight Lt. W. T. Day and Pilot Officer D. R. Stewart took off in their single engine plane in Mesopotamia. They were on a desert reconnaissance that was estimated to take four hours. When they failed to return, it was assumed that they had crashed. In those days, there were few enemy aircraft who might have shot them down. But the next day, their plane was found in the desert. They had obviously landed and there was plenty of petrol in the tank. The engine started as soon as it was tried. There were no signs of bullet holes in the plane, which might explain why it had landed.

In the soft sand there were boot marks where the two fliers had jumped down from the aeroplane, and these went on for about 40 yards. Then, they simply stopped. No sign of the men or their skeletons was ever found.

Missing Children

One case that seems to invite the UFO abduction explanation took place in 1906 and involved three children. The writer Harold Wilkins, described it in a book called *Mysteries: Solved and Unsolved* (1959). This is what he has to say.

The author of this book himself took part in a search by scores of people, in the summer of 1906, of some lonely fields . . . . In [this] case, which happened on a June day in a big pasture, locally known as the 'Forty Acres', close to a locomotive engine-shed of the old Midland Railway and marshalling yards of the Great Western line then a mile outside the city of Gloucester, three children, a boy about ten and his two sisters, aged three and five, went into this field and never returned. For three days and nights, scores of people, including the cleaners from the locomotive shed, searched every inch of the 'Forty Acres'. (Today the site of the field has almost been lost, for on it stands a big records department of the RAF, small factories, and some new streets and many houses.) We paid particular attention to the north-east corner of the field, where the pasture was bordered by tall, old elms, a thick hedge of thorn and bramble, and a deep ditch separating it from a cornfield. Every inch was probed with sticks, and not a stone left unturned in the ditch. Had a dead dog been dumped there, he would certainly have been found. Not a trace of the missing children was found.

The affair was headlined by all the newspapers, and quite large sums for the aid of the family were collected from the readers of Sunday newspapers. The father,

Thomas Vaughan, was a rather uncouth railway goods guard, or brake man, who (said his neighbours), was soon 'rolling in money' sent to him in every post by sympathisers. Indeed, a special staff had to be put on at the local Post Office, in order to deal with the numerous postal orders he received. The vicar of his parish called on him, only to be told by Vaughan that he 'wanted no b - - - - - - parsons a rappin' at his door,' nor any sympathy from them.

The mystery had been given up both by local police and public as beyond solution, when, just after six a.m., on the fourth day (they started early in those times), a ploughman went to work in a nearby corn-field, and looking over the hedge, saw, in the bottom of the ditch, the three missing children asleep! He informed the police and claimed a share of the reward which had been collected by the *News of the World* for anyone who could throw a light on the mystery. He was clearly entitled to it. But a local bigwig, who was then superintendent of the Gloucester City Police refused to hand over to the ploughman any share of the money. He insinuated that, in his official view, the man had probably kidnapped the three children and held them in order to collect the newspaper reward.

The poor ploughman lived in a cottage, one of about a dozen others, in a hamlet called Coney Hill, and it was really quite impossible for him to have done what the Gloucester Police superintendent had alleged, or insinuated, without his neighbors, all of the provincial sort, who knew all and more about their next door neighbor's private affairs, being at once aware of the presence, in the man's cottage, of three hidden children about whom a national hue and cry had started. Moreover, there was the trifling circumstance that the farmer, by whom he was employed, would certainly have become aware that his fieldworker had absented himself from his work in order to remove the children; for the farmer closely supervised the work in the field, harvest time being near. The ploughman never received a penny of the reward, and became slandered into the bargain, with the local police by no means playing the slander down. Nehemiah Philpott, the police superintendent thus had the last word in the affair. He died years ago.

One of the missing children is still alive. (They may all be; for the longevity of folk in Gloucestershire is well known to the statisticians.) He is now a man in his late sixties, and at the end of the Second World War, someone who remembered this case in 1906, questioned him. Vaughan replied that he had not the slightest recollection, nor had ever had, of what happened between the time when he and his sisters were missing in the 'Forty Acre' Field, and when they were found asleep in the ditch. If this be so, here, again, *is the characteristic of the amnesia which marks these phenomena*. [My italics.] It may be added that there was no financial incentive for anyone to kidnap these three children, and, moreover, the reward offered by the newspaper had been offered only after they were missing. No one, indeed, spoke of kidnapping until the local police superintendent put it forward as a too obvious solution. The affair remained a mystery; for who, in a country town like Gloucester in 1906, had ever heard of the phenomenon of 'teleportation', or would have had the ghost of an idea of what the outlandish word meant?

I have underlined the phrase about amnesia because Wilkins obviously feels that it is common in such cases. There can be no doubt that if he were alive today, he would regard UFO abduction as the most likely explanation.

In fact, Wilkins himself was the author of two early books about "Flying Saucers". But those were the days – during the 1950s – when those who did not dismiss them as mere hallucinations believed that they were probably solid craft from some other planet. The only mystery was why these visitors from space, having travelled so far, failed to make themselves known to the people of the earth.

Since the late 1960s, it has become slowly apparent that UFOs – or at least most of them – are nothing as straightforward as this. People who have interacted with the UFO phenomenon report strange men in black (who may disappear quite suddenly), objects that fly across rooms, and cases where the "aliens" seem to be able to read the minds of human beings. Many stories of "close encounters" between human beings and aliens seem so illogical and confusing that it is tempting to dismiss them as hysteria. Yet the sheer volume of evidence makes this virtually impossible.

The truth is that the "aliens" often behave more like ghosts or poltergeists – or even fairies or hobgoblins – than solid living creatures. There is a distinct touch of the "supernatural" about most UFO phenomena.

So, although there may be a perfectly natural explanation for the disappearance and reappearance of the Vaughan children in 1906, the facts seem to suggest that there may be an explanation which is not in accord with our usual scientific view of the universe. It will be worth bearing this in mind when considering some of the other strange vanishings in this book.

2

Abducted by Fairies?

There is a pamphlet in the British Museum signed "J. Cotham" dating from the year 1678. It claims to be an account of the abduction of an Irishman called Dr Moore by a troop of fairies at an inn at Dromgreagh in County Wicklow.

The doctor and his three friends – who all signed the pamphlet as witnesses to the occurrences it describes – were eating supper when the doctor began to tell his friends how he had been abducted by fairies as a child on a number of occasions, and rescued by the local witch, who had performed some kind of magic. At this point, the three witnesses saw Dr Moore staring in terror across the room, declaring that the fairies had come back for him. As they watched, Dr Moore was pulled out of his chair by invisible hands, out of the door, and out into the night.

The innkeeper advised that the best thing to do was to consult the local witch. When they told her the story, she had no doubt that the doctor had been abducted by the local fairies, and that he was now undoubtedly in their home in a nearby wood. She would do her best to rescue him by means of a spell, but its success depended upon the doctor refusing any food or drink while he was with the fairies. If he *did* partake of their hospitality, it would be possible to rescue him but he would almost certainly sicken and die. She proceeded to weave her spells, after which the three men returned to the inn.

The next morning, Dr Moore appeared, dishevelled and exhausted. He said that he had been taken off to the underground home of the faëry and that they had offered him food and drink. But whenever he had taken it from them, it had suddenly been dashed out of his hand by some unseen force. It seemed that the old witch's spell had summoned invisible allies.

Fairies, Poltergeists or Witches

Inevitably, we regard such tales as silly inventions – although it is difficult to understand why three witnesses took the trouble to set down their account of what had happened if the whole thing was a hoax. Our scepticism is due to the fact that we think of fairies as tiny winged creatures of the kind who flutter across the stage on wires in *Peter Pan*.

But we may be being premature. In the summer of 1897, the poet W. B. Yeats went to stay at Coole Park in Galway with Lady Augusta Gregory, and the two of them began collecting fairy stories from the local peasantry. Yeats had already compiled two collections of Irish myths and fairy tales, and obviously wrote about them with his tongue in his cheek. What startled him when he talked to peasants in the company of Lady Gregory was that they told such precise and circumstantial stories about fairies, and that so

The Irish lyric poet, W. B. Yeats

many of them claimed to have seen them. It seemed highly unlikely that they were all simply liars – or that they had allowed their imaginations to run away with them.

In his autobiography, G. K. Chesterton supports Yeats, "It is the fact that it is not abnormal men like artists, but normal men like peasants, who have born witness a thousand times to such things: it is the farmers who see the fairies. It is the agricultural laborer who calls a spade a spade who also calls a spirit a spirit; it is the woodcutter with no axe to grind . . . . who will say he saw a man hang on the gallows, and afterwards hang round it as a ghost." And he goes on to say about Yeats, "He was the real original rationalist who said that fairies stand to reason. He staggered the materialists by attacking their abstract materialism with a completely concrete mysticism; 'Imagination!', he would say with withering contempt, 'There wasn't much imagination when Farmer Hogan was dragged out of bed and thrashed like a sack of potatoes – that they did, they had 'um out,' (the Irish accent warming with scorn), 'They had 'um out and thumped 'um; and that's not the sort of thing that a man wants to imagine.'"

Now the first thing that will strike readers about these fairies who thrashed Farmer Hogan is that they seem to be behaving very much like the traditional poltergeist. In a famous case in 1817, a farmer named John Bell (who lived with his family in Robertson County, Tennessee, with his wife Lucy and nine children), was virtually beaten to death by poltergeists. It began, as poltergeist cases normally do, with noises of knocking and scraping behind the walls. Then the poltergeist began throwing stones, knocking over chairs, and pulling hair when the family was asleep. The daughter, Betsy, was attacked all the time. There would be a sharp slapping noise and her cheek would go red. After a week or so, the poltergeist began to speak, usually using bad language. It could also be benevolent – at Betsy's birthday party it said, "I have a surprise for you," and materialized a basket of fruit, including oranges and bananas, which it claimed had come from the West Indies.

John Bell finally became the center of it's attentions. It would follow him and use foul language, and strike him so hard in the face that he was stunned and had to sit down. His body would go into convulsions and his shoes would fly off every time he raised a foot to walk. On one occasion, the poltergeist – which had by then become known as "the Bell witch" – claimed to have given him a large dose of some sleeping medicine while he was asleep and the bottle appeared mysteriously in the medicine cupboard. When the cat was given a small dose, it jumped and whirled around, then fell down dead. And the following day, December 20th, 1820, Bell himself died.

It should be remembered that the case occurred several decades before the Americans discovered "spiritualism", and that at that time no one was interested in table rapping or playing with the Ouija board. So the case was observed – by dozens of neighbors over several years – simply as a case of malevolent witchcraft.

Now it is true that poltergeists only seldom indulge in physical attacks – such as pulling hair or slapping the face. More often, a heavy object will fly across the room with enough force to kill someone if struck on the head, and then, at the last moment, it will quite suddenly turn in another direction. The fact that these objects sometimes turn a full ninety degrees at great speed, implies that they are actually being held by some invisible force and not simply thrown. The case of John Bell is one of the few on record in which a poltergeist seems to have actually harmed anyone – and even then, the poltergeist was only the indirect cause of his death.

Early in the twentieth century, it became fashionable to believe that poltergeists were simply some strange activity due to the unconscious minds of disturbed teenagers. The phenomenon was called "psychokinesis" – a form of "mind over matter." This view was strengthened by Freud's theory of the unconscious mind, and his view that all neurosis is due to sexual repression. The fact that adolescents often seem to be the "focus" of poltergeist activity seemed to confirm this idea – since their bodies were going through the changes that bring sexual adulthood. But in recent years, an increasing number of psychical researchers have come to take the view that poltergeists are precisely what they claim to be – spirits.

Here I should add a personal digression. As a writer on "occult" subjects, I had always accepted the view that poltergeists are due to the unconscious minds of disturbed teenagers. When presenting a programme about poltergeists for television, I met a girl in the BBC television canteen whose flatmate was suffering from the attentions of a poltergeist – her clothes would vanish, her belongings would disappear and then turn up in another place, and occasionally the bedclothes would be pulled off her bed. I told the girl to assure her flatmate that the poltergeist was actually created by her own unconscious mind and that there was no "spirit" involved.

26

In November 1930, a trapper named Joe Labelle approached a small Eskimo village on the shore of Lake Anjikuni (500 miles north of Churchill), in north-eastern Canada.

Expecting to be greeted by the Eskimos, whom he knew well, Labelle was puzzled when there was no reply to his shout. The whole village was silent. He spent an hour looking for some sign of life but the village was deserted. He looked inside the tents, made of caribou skin, but they were all deserted – although in one tent there was a sealskin garment for a small child, with the ivory needle still sticking in it. He also found a number of burnt-out fires, with cooking pots containing food still hanging over them. On the beach there were three kayaks, and they looked so torn by the waves that he judged they had been there for several months.

Mounties who came to investigate were puzzled to find several rifles in the tents. Rifles are prized possessions and no Eskimo would deliberately abandon them. A hundred yards from the camp, the remains of seven dogs, tied to tree stumps, were found – all had died of starvation.

What was even more puzzling was an open grave, with the pile of stones which – by Eskimo custom – should have covered it, neatly stacked beside it. Some member of the tribe who had been buried there had been removed – and presumably taken with the Eskimos when they left.

Skilled trackers failed to find any sign of the missing tribe. And no one ever found any clue to why more than 30 people had left so hurriedly.

In 1980, I was commissioned to write a book about poltergeists, and heard about a particularly fascinating case in Pontefract in Yorkshire. It occurred in the late 1960s, and the entity was highly destructive – the family had a large tea-chest full of broken crockery which the poltergeist had hurled across the room.

I went up to Pontefract to interview the family, who were called Pritchard and who lived in a housing estate off Chequerfield in Pontefract. Their house apparently stood on the site of an old gallows on a hill top.

The "haunting" started with a fine gray powder which drifted down through the air in the lounge like snow forming a white layer all over the furniture. Then water began to come up through the kitchen floor, and when the toilet was flushed a greenish foam rushed out. Then the poltergeist began slamming doors, shaking furniture with strange vibrations, and breaking crockery. Soon the Pritchards' daughter, Diane, became the "focus" of the poltergeist's attentions. She found it hard to sleep sometimes – the bedclothes would be pulled off the bed, the mattress turned upside down so that she flew out onto the floor, and the room was filled with a drumming sound which kept everybody awake. One day, a brass crucifix shot off the mantelpiece and suddenly stuck in the middle of Diane's back refusing to be pulled off. The phenomena reached a climax when the poltergeist grabbed Diane by the throat and proceeded to drag her up the stairs. When the family managed to drag her free, her throat was covered with red finger marks.

It was Diane was describing her experience of the poltergeist to me that I suddenly knew with absolute total conviction that this was not her own unconscious mind. It was undoubtedly some kind of spirit. In fact, a number of the family had seen a ghostly form (rather like a monk) around the house, and there had been a local monastery close by. The family had come to the conclusion that the monk they saw had been hanged on the gallows where their house stood, and that he was now haunting them.

The disturbances in Pontefract came to an end as quickly as they began. It simply went away. But even when I went there, ten years later, the Pritchards still had tape recordings of their ghostly visitor making tremendous banging noises, while neighbors came in and described to us, in circumstantial detail, exactly what they had seen. There could be no doubt that the whole thing was genuine. And there was no doubt in my mind that whatever entity was causing the trouble was using the adolescent energies of the two children, Phillip and Diane – the hauntings started when they reached adolescence.

I must admit that I was unhappy about the idea of accepting the reality of spirits, but the evidence all pointed in that direction. And when I came to write the book about the poltergeist, and to record dozens of cases over the centuries, it became clear to me that the poltergeist is some kind of mischievous spirit that (under certain circumstances) can make use of the energies of human beings, particularly those who are in a state of emotional disturbance. They seem to be the juvenile delinquents of the spirit world and to enjoy causing trouble. They are far more frequent than anybody supposes – there is probably a poltergeist disturbance going on within ten miles of where you are reading this book. When I enquired about the area where I live, I found several of them, all in full swing.

I cannot claim that all this changed my view of life. I came to accept the existence of spirits in the same way that you might accept the existence of badgers at the bottom of your garden, or rats in the coal shed. In many cases, it seems fairly clear that they are the spirits of dead people. In a famous case that took place in Enfield, a medium investigating the disturbances commented that the house seemed to be full of the whole contents of the graveyard next door. And since fairies, ghosts, poltergeists, "vampires", and even UFO phenomena seem to have something in common, I would suggest that we may be dealing with the same spirit delinquents making a nuisance of themselves.

Abduction by Fairies

Now one of Yeats's closest friends was a remarkable Irish poet and mystic called George Russell, who wrote books under the name of AE. In his late teens, after suffering severe inner conflicts, Russell began to "see visions". He describes how, drowsing on a hillside on a warm summer day, "the heart of the hills was opened to me." Then he began seeing creatures that he recognised as fairies – not the fairies of English folklore, looking like Tinker-bell, but semitransparent beings who usually glowed with a curious light. "The first . . . . I saw I remember very clearly . . . . there was a dazzle of light, and then I saw that this came from the heart of a tall figure with a body apparently shaped out of half transparent or opalescent air, and throughout the body ran a radiant electrical fire, to which the heart seemed the center.

Around the head of this being and through its waving luminous hair, which was blown all about the body like living strands of gold, there appear flaming wing-like auras. From the being itself light seemed to stream outwards in every direction; and the effect left on me after the vision was of extraordinary likeness, joyousness or ecstasy." Yeats had no doubt whatever that his friend's visions were of nature-spirits or "elementals", and that these elementals are what simple country folk have always called fairies.

Now Yeats and Russell had a young friend whose ambition was to become a scholar. His name was Evans Wentz, and he was to become well known in later years as the translater of many religious books of Tibet. But it was Yeats and Russell who persuaded Wentz that it would be worth his while to start his career by talking to ordinary country folk about the belief in fairies. The result was a remarkable work called *The Fairy-Faith in Celtic Countries* (1911). Wentz did what Yeats and Lady Gregory had done – in June 1908 he began to travel around Wales, Ireland, Scotland, Cornwall and Brittany, knocking on the doors of cottages and asking questions about "the little folk". Like Yeats, he was astonished to discover how many people took the existence of fairies completely for granted – even educated people.

Now although Wentz had the academic temperament, he was not stupid enough to try to dismiss the fairy-faith as some kind of superstitious delusion. To begin with, many of the people he interviewed told him about their own personal experiences of fairies. For example, at Pentraeth near Anglesey, a Mr Gwilyn Jones remarked, "It always was and still is the opinion that the *Tylwyth Teg* (fairies) are a race of spirits. Some people think them small in size, but the one my mother saw was ordinary human size." Wentz hastened to see Mr Jones's mother who told him, "I was coming home at about half past ten at night from Cemaes . . . . where I was in service, when there appeared just before me a very pretty young woman of ordinary size. I had no fear, and when I came up to her I put out my hand to touch her, but my hand and arm went right through her form. I could not understand this, and so tried to touch her repeatedly with the same result; there was no solid substance in the body, yet it remained beside me, and was as beautiful a young lady as I ever saw. When I reached the door of the house where I was to stop, she was still with me. Then I said 'goodnight' to her. No response being made I asked, 'why do you not speak?' and at this she disappeared."

Wentz came to the conclusion that the forces of nature in remote country areas "impress man and awaken in him some unfamiliar part of himself – call it the Subconscious Self, the Subliminal Self, the Ego, or what you will – which gives him the unusual power to know and to feel invisible or psychical influences. What is there, for example, in London, or Paris, or Berlin, or New York to awaken the intuitive power of man, that subconsciousness deep-hidden in him?"

This seems to be confirmed by a man called William Jones, "who declared that he had seen the *Tylwyth Teg* in the Aberglaslyn Pass near Beddgelert, was publicly questioned about them in Bethel Chapel by Mr Griffiths, the minister; and he explained before the congregation that the Lord had given him a special vision which enabled him to see the *Tylwyth Teg*, and that, therefore, he had seen them time after time as little men playing along the river in the Pass." In short, William Jones is simply what we would now call a born "psychic", someone who can see things that other people cannot see.

The curious thing about the thousands of ghost-sightings in the records of the Society for Psychical Research is that, again and again, a ghost may appear to a group of people, and only certain persons in that group are able to see it. Wentz's book is full of accounts of fairy abductions – there are no less than forty references to them. One countryman from County Sligo gave Wentz the following account. "When I was a young man I often used to go out in the mountains over there (pointing out of the window in their direction) to fish for trout, or to hunt; and it was in January on a cold, dry day while carrying my gun that I and a friend with me as we were walking around Ben Bulben, saw one of the *gentry* for the first time. I knew who it was, for I had heard the *gentry* described ever since I could remember; and this one was dressed in blue with a head-dress adorned with what seemed to be frills." (Wentz adds that another Irish seer – undoubtedly Russell – thinks this head-dress should really be described as an aura.) "When he came up to us, he said to me in a sweet and silvery voice, 'the seldomer you come to this mountain the better. A young lady here wants to take you away.' Then he told us not to fire off our guns, because the *gentry* dislike being disturbed by the noise. And he seemed like a soldier of the *gentry* on guard. As we were leaving the mountains, he told us not to look back, and we didn't. Another time I was alone trout-fishing in nearly the same region when I heard a voice say, 'it is – bare-footed and fishing.' Then there came a whistle like music and a noise like the beating of a drum, and soon one of *gentry* came and talked with me for half an hour. He said, 'Your mother will die in eleven months, and do not let her die unanointed.' And she did die within eleven months. As he was going away he warned me, 'You must be in the house before sunset. Do not delay! Do not delay! They can do nothing to you until I get back in the castle.' As I found out afterwards, he was going to *take* me, but hesitated because he did not want to leave my mother alone. After these warnings I was always afraid to go to the mountains . . . ."

In many cases, "take" seems to be a euphemism for "die". "We were told as children, that, as soon as night fell, the fairies from Rath Rangles Town would form in a procession, across Tara road, pass round certain bushes which have not been disturbed for ages and join the host of industrious folk, the red fairies. We were afraid, and our nurses always brought us home before the advent of the fairy procession. One of the passes used by this procession happened to be between two mud-wall houses; and it is said that a man went out of one of these houses at the wrong time, for when he was found he was dead; the fairies had *taken* him because he interfered with their procession." Another country-man remarks that fairies are generally believed to be spirits of the dead. The man who had encountered the *gentry* on Ben Bulben told Wentz, "They are able to appear in different forms. One once appeared to me, and seemed only four feet high, and stoutly built. He said, 'I am bigger than I appear to you now. We can make the old young, the big small, the small big.' One of their women told all the secrets of my family. She said that my brother in Australia would travel much and suffer hardships, all of which came true; and foretold that my nephew, then about two years old, would become a great clergyman in America, and that is what he is now."

Wentz interviewed George Russell at length, and Russell made some very important points. He emphasized that the fairy-folk were not seen in the ordinary physical sense. "In seeing these beings of which we speak, physical eyes may be open or closed: mystical beings in their own world and nature are never seen with the physical eyes." Now it is very interesting to learn how Russell developed his "visionary" faculty. It was a quite deliberate discipline. He began by trying to remember his own past in detail, and admitted that he found it very hard work. But with a great deal of practise, he was gradually able to remember all kinds of things, and conjure them up as if they had happened an hour earlier. This is important. In 1933, a young neurosurgeon named Wilder Penfield made an interesting discovery. He was performing a brain operation on a patient who was wide awake (since the brain has no nerves it does not feel pain), and he happened to touch the temporal cortex – the seat of memory – with a probe that carried a weak electric current. As long as the probe was in contact, the patient experienced a memory of childhood – a memory so precise in detail that it was like reliving it. Penfield had accidentally caused some of the patient's "memory tapes" to play back. Each contact of the probe brought back *one single* memory in minute detail. Most of us have no ability to establish contact with these "memory tapes" although a sudden smell or taste may bring back vividly some memory of the past. Now what Russell proved, to his own satisfaction, is that by making considerable efforts to recall his own past, he could gradually get better and better at it. His unconscious mind began to understand what he wanted, and began to throw its weight behind his efforts.

Psychic Forces

It was after he had become skilled in recreating memories from his own past that Russell realised that he was also able to see "other realities". Asked by Wentz under what conditions he saw fairies, he said, "I have seen them most frequently after being away from a city or town for a few days. The whole West coast of Ireland from Donegal to Kerry seems charged with a magical power, and I find it easiest to see while I am there. I have always found it comparatively easy to see visions while at ancient monuments like New Grange and Dowth, because I think such places are naturally charged with psychical forces, and were for that reason made use of long ago as sacred places. I usually find it possible to throw myself into the mood of seeing; but sometimes visions have forced themselves upon me." Now what Russell is saying here, in about 1908, is what would now be generally accepted by millions of people who are interested in so called "ley lines". These are lines of force in the earth, possibly ordinary earth magnetism. One famous "ley" runs from the east coast of England all the way down to St Michael's Mount in Cornwall, and it has been noted that there are an enormous number of churches named for St Michael along this ley line. Dowsers – water diviners – can actually detect these ley lines with their dowsing rods, particularly in the area of standing stones, like Stonehenge. And they would agree that, at certain points, the earth appears to be exceptionally highly charged with some unknown force. Such spots have always been chosen as sacred sites – dating back long before Christianity. Moreover, many Christian churches have been built on the sites of Pagan temples, obviously because someone recognised that there was some kind of force in the earth itself. So everything that Russell said here would make sense to a modern student of ley lines.

Shining Beings

Wentz asked Russell if he could describe the shining beings, and Russell said, "It is very difficult to give any intelligible description of them. The first time I saw them with great vividness I was lying on a hill-side alone in the west of Ireland, in County Sligo: I had been listening to music in the air, and to what seemed to be the sound of bells, and was trying to understand these aerial clashings in which wind seemed to break upon wind in an everchanging musical silvery sound. Then the space before me grew luminous, and I began to see one beautiful being after another." Russell called the faery the *Sidhe*, and commented, "The beings whom I called the *Sidhe*, I divide, as I have seen them, into two great classes: those which are shining, and those which are opalescent and seem lit up by a light within themselves. The shining beings appear to be lower in the hierarchies; the opalescent beings are more rarely seen, and appear to hold the positions of great chiefs or princes among the tribes of Dana." He explains to Wentz that, "the opalescent beings seem to be about fourteen feet in stature . . . . the shining beings seem to be about our own stature or just a little taller."

Russell stated that he had often been with other people when he had seen the *Sidhe*, and that they had also seen them. This gave Wentz an opportunity to check up on what Russell was telling him, and he got Russell to introduce him to three people who had been with him on such occasions – all of them verified that they had both seen the *Sidhe*. On one occasion, Russell and a friend were some distance apart when they saw the *Sidhe*, and they hurried together to tell one another – only to discover that they had both seen exactly the same thing. Wentz adds that he has spoken with a number of reliable people who have seen the *Sidhe*. "One is a member of the Royal Irish Academy, and the other is the wife of a well-known Irish historian; and both of them testified to having likewise had collective visions of *Sidhe* beings in Ireland."

Gentle Folk

As already stated, the word *taken* seems a euphemism for death. An old man named Neil Colton (known in County Donegal as a seer) told Wentz, "One day, just before sunset in midsummer, and I a boy then, my brother and cousin and myself were gathering bilberries up by the rocks at the back of here, when all at once we heard music. We hurried round the rocks, and there we were within a few hundred feet of six or eight of the *gentle folk*, and they were dancing. When they saw us, a little woman dressed all in red came running out from them towards us, and she struck my cousin across the face with what seemed to be a green rush. We ran for home as hard as we could, and when my cousin reached the house she fell dead. Father saddled the horse and went for Father Ryan. When Father Ryan arrived, he put a stole about his neck and began praying over my cousin and reading psalms and striking her with the stole; and in that way brought her back. He said if she had not caught hold of my brother, she would have been *taken* for ever." But, as the school master explained to Wentz, there was also a wide spread belief in the stealing of children from cradles, and replacing them with a weakly or shrivelled fairy child.

Changelings

A farmer named James Caugherty told Wentz a story (which I am abridging because it is too long to quote) of a boy called Robbie, with whom he played as a child. One evening, Robbie came to his house to borrow candles, and on his way home was followed by a small boy and a little woman. He ran as fast as he could, but they ran after him. As he staggered over the threshold of his house, he was unable to speak, his hands and his feet looked different, and his fingernails were far longer than they had been. The boy's mother assumed that the shock of being chased had caused her son to lose his mind. But James Caugherty's father was certain that this boy was not Robbie at all, but the boy who had been with the old woman. He persuaded the mother to send for a doctor who was said to have the power of "doing charms." She sent a messenger to the doctor explaining the circumstances, and just as the messenger returned home the doctor's charms were apparently successful, because when the woman returned from opening the door her son Robbie was there once again, looking perfectly normal. Robbie explained how the woman and the boy had chased him, and that as he reached his own door, he was conscious of being taken away by them. He said he had no memory whatever of what had happened while he was away.

It is interesting to notice the parallel between such stories of "changelings", and the fact that modern UFO abductions often seem to involve women who have babies planted in their wombs by the "aliens", and then later removed. Budd Hopkins, the New York expert on abductions, is convinced that most alien abduction is concerned with genetic experiments, and that the aliens perform these experiments in an attempt to save their race from dying out. The parallel with the *Sidhe* is obvious. In his book *Witnessed* (1996), Budd Hopkins writes, "Everything I have learned in twenty years of research into the UFO abduction phenomenon leads me to conclude that the aliens' central purpose is not to teach us about taking better care of the environment. Instead, all of the evidence points to their having been here to carry out a complex breeding experiment in which they seem to be working to create a hybrid species, a mix of human and alien characteristics. A careful reading of the various witnesses' accounts suggests that here, as in many earlier cases, reproductive issues appear far more frequently than alien ecological concerns." And he goes on to speak about two of the abductees, a male and female, whose cases he has presented at length, and how they were "bonded" during an earlier abduction experience, and how they have both come to suspect that the son to whom she subsequently gave birth may not be the child of her husband.

If all the talk about fairies and changelings seems preposterous, then consider the following comments by Doctor Richard F. Haines, who specialises in recovering the memory of people who believe that they may have been abducted. Most abductions, Haines says, involves seven or more of the following experiences:

"An alert – something that diverts attention away from whatever an individual may be doing before the abduction.

"Capture (and the loss of self-will) – abductees often report that they felt lured as though they 'couldn't resist.'

"Abduction – abductees may travel through a window, a door, or a wall. Typically, they report arriving at an enclosure or an unknown environment.

"A tour – abductees often report that their captors show them around the spacecraft or lead them through passageways or rooms, where they notice unusual lighting or advanced technology.

"A personal examination – alien beings may conduct a careful study of the abductee's body, mind, or spirit.

"Communication and messages – researchers are especially interested in accounts of telepathic or auditory communications, as well as written information to or from the abductee, always in the abductee's own language.

"Return to original location – abductees are returned to the same place they were before the abduction.

"Aftermath – abductees commonly report physical, psychological and spiritual changes within a few days after their abduction.

"Post-event – other effects appear later, which may not seem to be clearly related to the claimed abduction, including job changes, having a child, or other major life events."

Writers like Budd Hopkins and John Mack agree that all this sounds so preposterous that any sensible person ought to dismiss it as a symptom of mild insanity. But when literally thousands of people report such experiences, it becomes clear that casual dismissal is the reaction of a closed mind. Now what is being suggested here is not that Celtic fairies were really "aliens", or that modern aliens are really fairies. The point is more interesting than that. What Russell is suggesting is that the chief mistake of modern man is to assume that this so-called "reality" that stretches around us is the only reality, and that we have no alternative to doing our best to spend our lives coping with this reality. Russell insists that there are, in fact, several levels of reality. They run parallel with this one, and so-called "fairies" can look *into* our reality just like visitors in an aquarium looking into the fish tanks. The fish also take their own reality for granted, and take no real interest at the human beings who peer in at them.

The point is made – with a great deal of humour – in a novel called *Sophie's World* by Jostein Gaarder (1994), a kind of children's story in which a little girl called Sophie finds a series of mysterious letters addressed to her in her letterbox. The first letter simply asks the question "who are you?", then the mysterious writer goes on to introduce her to philosophy and to the kind of questions that philosophers ask. She suddenly feels as if she has been shaken awake from a deep sleep. Gaarder writes, "She had never thought so hard before! She was no longer a child – but she wasn't really grown up either. Sophie realised that she had already begun to crawl down into the cosy rabbit's fur, the very same rabbit that had been pulled from the top hat of the universe. But the philosopher had stopped her. He – or was it a she? – had grabbed her by the back of the neck and pulled her up again to the tip of the fur where she had played as a child. And there, on the outermost tips of the fine hairs, she was once again seeing the world as if for the first time.

"The philosopher had rescued her. No doubt about it. The unknown letter writer had saved her from the triviality of everyday existence.

"When Mom got home at five o'clock, Sophie dragged her into the living room and pushed her into an armchair.

" 'Mom – don't you think it's astonishing to be alive?' she began.

"Her mother was so surprised that she didn't answer at first, Sophie was usually doing her homework when she got home.

" 'I suppose I do – sometimes,' she said.

" 'Sometimes? Yes, but – don't you think it's aston-ishing that the world *exists* at all?'

" 'Now look, Sophie. Stop talking like that.'

" 'Why? Perhaps you think the world is quite normal?'

" 'Well, isn't it? More or less, anyway.'

"Sophie saw that the philosopher was right. Grownups took the world for granted. They had let themselves be lulled into the enchanted sleep of their humdrum existence once and for all."

George Russell is saying much the same thing. He is saying that modern man – particularly the city dweller – has decided to close his mind to whole levels of reality.

We might conclude this chapter with the interesting cautionary tale that makes the same point.

The Little People

In 1920, the British public was intrigued to learn of new scientific evidence that seemed to place belief in "the little people" on an altogether solider foundation. The front cover of the Christmas issue of the *Strand* magazine announced, "An Epoch-Making event . . . . described by Conan Doyle." Facing the opening page of the article was a photograph of a teenage girl in a white cotton dress, sitting in a grassy field and holding out a hand to a dancing gnome. Another photograph showed a younger girl gazing mildly into the camera over a group of four cavorting fairies, complete with gossamer wings. The caption under the first photograph stated, "This picture and the even more extraordinary one of the fairies on page 465 are two of the most astounding photographs ever published. How they were taken is fully described in Sir Arthur Conan Doyle's article." This was not a seasonal joke. Doyle and his fellow investigators were convinced that the two photographs virtually proved the existence of "the little people." Resulting controversy was to remain unsettled for the next sixty years.

The girls in the photograph were Elsie Wright and Frances Griffiths, and they lived in the village of Cottingley, in Yorkshire. They had taken the photographs three-and-a-half years earlier in the summer of 1917, and had consistently claimed, often in the face of extremely sceptical cross examination, that the photographs were of real fairies.

In April 1917, ten-year-old Frances Griffiths moved to the village of Cottingley with her mother Annie, from South Africa. She later claimed that she soon realised there were fairies in the fields around her home, especially in the local beck (stream), which ran down a steep-sided dell at the bottom of her garden. She later described the first time she had seen a fairy down by the stream, "One evening after school, I went down to the beck to a favorite place – the willow overhanging the stream . . . . then a willow leaf started shaking violently – just one. I'd seen it happen before – there was no wind, and it was odd that one leaf should shake . . . . as I watched a small man, all dressed in green, stood on the branch with the stem of the leaf in his hand, which he seemed to be shaking at something he was looking at. I didn't dare move for fear of frightening him. He looked straight at me and disappeared."

Any of Wentz's interviewees would have accepted this account without raising an eyebrow. But Frances was living in common sense Yorkshire, and she decided to tell no one for fear of being laughed at. She explained how, as the summer wore on, she had become increasingly fascinated by the stream and how she would spend hours "fairy watching" in the dell. One day, when she arrived home soaked from a fall in the stream, her mother and her Aunt Polly pressed hard for an explanation. Their eyes widened when Frances replied, "I go to see the fairies." At this point, to the surprise of the two women, Frances's cousin, seventeen-year-old Elsie Wright, came to her defence and insisted that she, too, had seen fairies. No amount of questioning could shake the girls' stories. According to Conan Doyle's article, it was this confrontation that convinced the two cousins that they must produce some indisputable evidence to make the grown-ups eat their words.

On a Saturday afternoon in July 1917, Elsie asked her father, Arthur Wright, if she could borrow his plate camera. He was understandably reluctant, since the camera was new and the plates expensive, but he eventually gave way. The girls hurried off to the stream and were back in half an hour. After tea, Arthur was coaxed into developing the plate. As the plate started to develop, he realised that it was a picture of Frances leaning on a bank that seemed to be scattered with sandwich papers. Then, to his amazement, he saw that the "papers" were tiny human forms with wings growing from their backs – they were apparently four dancing fairies!

The girls' mothers didn't know quite what to think. Both had recently become interested in Theosophy – the movement founded by Madame Blavatsky, who taught that behind the real world of everyday reality there was an invisible world peopled by spiritual beings, including nature spirits or fairies. (George

Russell was also a member of the Theosophical Society.) But Arthur Wright refused to be taken in. He was convinced that the fairies were paper cut-outs.

In August, the girls borrowed the camera again; this time they returned with a picture of Elsie sitting in a field watching a dancing gnome. They explained that they often saw gnomes in the field just above the stream. After this, in the interest of peace and quiet. Arthur refused further loans of his camera. But several prints were made of each plate.

After the war – a year later – Frances's mother and her Aunt Polly went to a local meeting of the Theosophical Society, and told the speaker about the photographs. He asked to see them, and copies were soon circulating. That was how the photographs came to appear in the *Strand Magazine* in 1920. The article became the talk of every London dinner table. The sceptics were outraged. But Conan Doyle, who had become convinced of the truth of Spiritualism during the war, insisted that there is nothing inherently unlikely in the idea of elementals or nature spirits. And so the controversy dragged on until it was finally forgotten. But in 1971, Elsie appeared on BBC television, and was asked if she would swear on the Bible that the photographs were not tricks. She replied after a pause, "I'd rather leave that open, if you don't mind." She seemed to be half admitting that there had been some kind of fraud.

A few years later, the Yorkshire psychical investigator Joe Cooper became interested in the case, and suggested making a television programme about it. Elsie and Frances, now old ladies, were photographed beside the stream where they had taken the pictures (they had taken another three in 1920), and once again the girls refused to say whether the pictures were genuine or a fake.

In 1977, a researcher named Fred Gettings, working on nineteenth-century fairy illustrations, came upon *Princess Mary's Gift Book*, published during the First World War to make money for the Work for Women fund. It contained a poem entitled "A Spell For a Fairy", by Alfred Noyes, illustrated by Claude Shepperson. Two of the fairies in the illustrations were virtually identical to the fairies in the first Cottingley photograph – it was merely there positions that had been reversed. The magician James Randi claimed that he had put the photograph through an image-enhancement process, and found that this revealed strings holding up the fairies. When Joe Cooper told Elsie about this, she merely laughed and pointed out that there was no way in the region of the stream where strings could have been tied. Finally, in September 1981, Frances made the admission that Cooper had been half-expecting for a long time. She told Cooper, "From where I was, I could see the hat-pins holding up the figures. I've always marvelled that anybody ever took it seriously." Cooper asked her, "What about the other four?" The reply was almost as astonishing as her first comment. "Three of them are fakes. The last one is genuine."

And so it looked as if the Cottingley fairy story had finally proved to be a fraud. But why had Frances insisted that the last of the photographs – showing "fairies and their sun bath", looking like a kind of sheath or cocoon made of gauze – was genuine? Was she merely trying to salvage a little of her self respect? Obviously, having confessed that the first four photographs were fakes, she could not expect anyone to believe that the last photograph was genuine.

Sir Arthur Conan Doyle

Frances died in 1986, Elsie in 1988. Both had fallen out with Joe Cooper for writing an article in which he revealed the fraud. But Joe Cooper feels that there is far more to say about the case of the Cottingley fairies. When Frances came to England at the age of ten, her cousin Elsie, six years her senior, had already had some interesting ghostly experiences. She insisted that when she was four she was regularly visited in bed by a woman who wore a tight dress buttoned up to her neck. And when she was six she woke up one night and called for a drink; when no one replied, she went downstairs, and found a strange man and woman in the house. She asked where her parents were and was told that they had gone out to play cards with the neighbors. Elsie said she wanted to go and find them, and the man opened the front door and led her out. Her parents – who were in fact playing cards with the neighbors – were startled to see her and even more startled to hear about the man and woman, for they had left the house empty. When they went to investigate, the house *was* empty. Frances had had no "psychic" experiences. But in the spring of 1918 she saw her first gnome. She had gone down to the stream after school and observed a phenomenon which she had often observed before. The shaking willow leaf, then a small man all dressed in green standing on the branch. After that, she claimed, she often saw little men wearing coats of grayish green and matching caps by the stream. She gradually reached the conclusion that the little men were engaged in some kind of purposeful activity, perhaps associated with helping plants to grow. Later, she began to see fairies, with and without wings. These were smaller than the elves; they had white faces and arms and often seemed to be holding some kind of meeting. Elsie apparently never saw the fairies. Both girls were later to admit to Joe Cooper that they had deliberately faked the first four photographs because they were angry about the total scepticism of the adults, and wanted to give them something to think about. Frances always maintained that the fairies were real, and in 1918 sent the first photograph to a friend in South Africa with the comment, "Elsie and I are very friendly with the beck Fairies. It's funny I never used to see them in Africa. It must be too hot for them there."

Sceptics will undoubtedly feel that Joe Cooper is showing himself to be painfully gullible when he accepts that both Elsie and Frances had had genuine "psychic" experiences. On the other hand, George Russell – and all of the other people interviewed by Evans Wentz – would take it for granted that Elsie and Frances were both telling the truth, and that it was their sheer irritation with the adults' refusal to believe them that led them to fake the first four photographs. When Joe Cooper decided to write his book *The Case of the Cottingley Fairies*, he originally included a chapter entitled "Other Sightings", consisting of an account of fairies related to him by various witnesses, and it becomes clear why he believed Frances. One man, a healer, told how he was sitting with a girl in Gibraltar, eating a sandwich, when it was snatched from him by "a little man about eighteen inches high." An eighty-year-old official of the Theosophical Society insisted that when he was a small boy he was often visited in bed by a green-clad gnome. Another old man described seeing a green-clad gnome about two feet high, walking along a path in a cornfield. Some young male students told how, when walking in a wood near Bradford, they saw fairies who were "circling and dancing" but who were invisible to the direct gaze; they could only be seen out of the corner of the eye. An elderly woman showed Cooper a photograph of a gnome seen through a frosty window; she claimed that she had come down one morning, seen the gnome, and rushed upstairs to get her camera. The photograph also shows diminutive white rabbits.

I was to write a chapter about fairies in my book *Poltergeist* (before Frances had confessed), and I also went to some trouble to find accounts of "real" fairies. I described being interviewed on television at the 1978 Edinburgh Festival by a man named Bobbie (whose surname I forgot to note), and how, in the pub next door, he told me casually that he had once seen a gnome standing on the pavement outside a convent gate and that it had "scared the hell out of him." My friend Marc Alexander, author of many books on the paranormal, told me a story of a friend in New Zealand named Pat Andrew, who claimed to have seen a pixie when he was six. Years later, after seeing a stage hypnotist, Marc and Pat began experimenting with hypnosis on each other. Marc had no doubt that Pat was genuinely hypnotised, and one day he decided to try and "regress" him to the age when he saw the pixie. The result was an amazing one-sided conversation that left Marc in no doubt whatever that, whether Andrew had really seen a pixie or not, he undoubtedly *believed* he had.

One of the most convincing accounts I know is of an encounter with a pixie as recounted by another friend,

the psychic Lois Bourne, in her book *Witch Among Us*.
Lois Bourne is an extremely sensible and down-to-earth
woman. And in her book, among many stories that
psychical researchers will find credible enough, she
tells a story that will obviously cause most readers to
doubt her truthfulness throughout. While on holiday
at a cottage at Crantock, in Cornwall, she met a
member of a "Wicca" coven and spent an evening at
her home. The woman's husband, Rob, asked her if she
would like to see a goblin, explaining that one appeared
among the rushes of the millstream at Treago Mill,
Cuberts Heath, every morning at sunrise; if she wanted
to see him, she had to be up early. The next morning
Lois and her husband Wilfred joined Rob at the mill
gate and they crept up the stream. Lois Bourne writes,
"I have never been able to decide, and still cannot
decide, whether I really saw that goblin, or if Rob
made me see it . . . . whatever it was, there, sitting on
a stone calmly washing his socks, was an elfin creature
with a red hat, green coat and trews, one yellow sock
on, and one in his tiny hands in the process of being
washed. I remember thinking at the time, in my sleepy,
befuddled, but practical way, 'what an atrocious color
combination.' Suddenly he saw us and he disappeared
. . . . 'Now do you believe me?' asked Rob." I have
known Lois Bourne for years. I may be gullible, and
she may be a liar, but I believe her. Besides, her
husband, Wilfred – who also saw it – verified the story.

As already mentioned at the beginning of this chapter, the poet W. B. Yeats had been convinced of the
existence of fairies every since he and Lady Gregory
went from door to door collecting information from
local peasants. They recorded these interviews in a

1920 book entitled *Visions and Beliefs*. Evans Wentz concludes his *Fairy-Faith in Celtic Countries* by acknowledging, "We seem to have arrived at a point . . . . where we can postulate scientifically . . . . the existence of such invisible intelligences as gods, genii, Daemons, all kinds of true fairies, and disembodied men." (By the latter he means ghosts.) And he goes on to cite the very sound evidence for the real existence of the poltergeist. The lesson seems to be that we should take seriously George Russell's insistence that the reality that surrounds us is only one of many realities.

3

Triangle of Death

The Bermuda Triangle ranks as one of the world's major mysteries. Yet this was not always so. Until the publication of The Bermuda Triangle, An Incredible Saga of Unexplained Disappearances *by Charles Berlitz, which became a bestseller in 1974, few people had ever heard of the Bermuda Triangle. Nowadays, it has become so notorious that there are a number of books with titles like* The Bermuda Triangle Mystery – Solved.

It is worth taking a longer and more careful look at the whole story.

As far as public awareness goes, it begins in February 1964, when an article called "The Deadly Bermuda Triangle" by Vincent Gaddis appeared in the American magazine *Argosy*. It began, "With a crew of thirty-nine, the tanker *Marine Sulphur Queen* began its final voyage on February 2, 1963, from Beaumont, Texas. Its announced destination was Norfolk, Virginia. Its actual destination was the unknown.

"The ship transported molten sulphur in heavily insulated steel tanks that were kept at 265 degrees by steel coils. The ship's operators, the Marine Transport Corporation of New York, said hauling sulphur was no more dangerous than hauling other cargoes.

"A routine radio message on the night of February 3 placed the 524-foot vessel near the Dry Tortugas in the Gulf of Mexico.

"Overdue on February 6, a search was launched. Planes took off from Coast Guard stations from Key West to Norfolk, and all available cutters were placed in service patrolling the coast.

"One search plane reported a 'yellow substance' on the sea 240 miles southeast of Jacksonville. A check by surface craft revealed that the substance was only seaweed. The search was abandoned on February 14. Five days later, a navy torpedo retriever found some debris and a lifejacket believed to be from the tanker, in the Florida Straits fourteen miles southeast of Key West. Nothing more has been found.

"The mysterious message that haunts the Atlantic off the Florida coast had claimed another victim. It strikes again and again – swallowing a ship or a plane, or leaving behind a derelict with no life aboard."

In fact, the disappearance of the *Sulphur Queen* is not a particularly good example of the mystery of the Bermuda Triangle. To begin with, Gaddis is inaccurate – the Board of Investigation documents reveal that the material recovered from the *Sulphur Queen* consisted of "eight lifejackets, five life rings, two name boards, one shirt, one piece of an oar, one storm oil can, one gasoline can, one cone buoy, and one fog horn . . . . the consensus of opinion was that possibly two life-jackets had been worn by persons, and that the shirt tied to a lifejacket had also been worn by a person. Numerous tears on the lifejacket indicated attack by predatory fish . . . ." So the cause of the tragedy is quite clear – the *Marine Sulphur Queen* blew up and sank quite unexpectedly. The Board of Investigation concluded that "agitation of the mass of sulphur acts to increase the amount of gasses liberated from solution. It is concluded that the sulphur was agitated as the vessel worked in the rough seas which she apparently encountered on this voyage . . . . it, therefore, follows that this agitation . . . . increased the volume of these gasses liberated from the molten sulphur . . . . although each tank had three vents, the fact that all tanks had a full load of cargo . . . . prevented a free flow of air. It appears that the venting arrangement was not too effective in clearing off these gases. In rough weather such as the vessel probably encountered on this voyage, the molten sulphur would pour out of the forward vents of the cargo tanks, at least partially obstructing these vents as the sulphur solidified." In other words, the problems of transporting molten sulphur (molten sulphur occupies far less volume than powdered sulphur) proved to be far more dangerous than the owners of the ship thought.

Gaddis went on to give a number of other examples of disappearances in the Bermuda Triangle – 24 four-engined Stratotanker jets which left Homestead, south of Miami, Florida on August 28, 1963, simply disappeared in clear weather with eleven men aboard. Gaddis adds, "The obvious explanation was that the tankers had collided in the air, but two days after the disappearance more debris was located – only it was found 160 miles from the first discovery. What happened remains a mystery."

In fact, this mystery was also solved by a writer called Lawrence David Kusche in a book called *The Bermuda Mystery Triangle – Solved*. He unearthed information that revealed that the so-called second patch of wreckage, 160 miles from the first, was actually found to consist of seaweed, driftwood and an old buoy. When he enquired at the Norton Air Force Base, where all accident documents are housed, he was told that "it was definitely established that a mid-air collision did occur between the aircraft in question." So yet another of Gaddis's examples proves to be less reliable than it sounds. Nevertheless, his article made it very clear that there had been so many disappearances in this Bermuda Triangle area that something very strange was going on.

Gaddis goes on to tell the story of one of the major mysteries of the Devil's Triangle. On the afternoon of December 5, 1945, five Avenger torpedo-bombers took off from Fort Lauderdale, Florida, for a routine two-hour patrol over the Atlantic. Flight 19 was commanded by Flight Leader Charles Taylor – the other four pilots were trainees, flying what is known as a "milk run", that is, a flight whose purpose is simply to increase their number of hours in the air without instructors. By 2.15 p.m. the planes were well over the Atlantic, and following their usual patrol route. The weather was warm and clear. At 3.45 p.m. the control tower received a message from Taylor, "This is an emergency. We seem to be off course. We cannot see land . . . . repeat . . . . we cannot see land."

"What is your position?"

"We're not sure of our position. We can't be sure where we are. We seem to be lost."

"Head due west," replied the tower.

"We don't know which way is west. Everything is wrong . . . . strange . . . . we can't be sure of any direction. Even the ocean doesn't look as it should."

The tower was perplexed; even if some kind of magnetic interference caused all five compasses to malfunction, the pilot should still be able to see the sun low in the western sky. Radio contact was now getting worse, restricting any messages to short sentences. At one point the tower picked up one pilot speaking to another, saying that all the instruments in his plane were "going crazy." At 4.00 p.m. the flight leader decided to hand over to someone else. At 4.24 p.m. the new leader told the tower, "We're not certain where we are." Unless the planes could find their way back over land during the next four hours, they would run out of fuel and be forced to land in the sea. At 6.27 p.m. a rescue mission was launched. A giant Martin Mariner flying-boat with a crew of thirteen, took off towards the last reported position of the flight. Twenty-three minutes later, the sky to the east was lit briefly by a bright orange flash. Neither the Martin Mariner nor the five Avengers ever returned.

What finally happened to the missing aircraft is certainly no mystery. The weather became worse during the course of that afternoon; ships reported "high winds and tremendous seas." Flight 19 must have run out of fuel, and landed in the sea. The mystery is *why* they became so completely lost and confused. Even if the navigation instruments had ceased to function, and visibility had become restricted to a few yards, it should have been possible to fly up over the clouds to regain their bearings. Gaddis goes on to mention that in 1947, an American Superfortress bomber vanished one hundred miles off Bermuda. An extensive search failed to find a trace. The authorities theorised that "a tremendous current of rising air in a cumulonimbus cloud might have disintegrated the bomber." Gaddis points out that, even so, there ought to have been some traces of it left in the sea.

He goes on to tell one of the most puzzling stories.

"The *Star Tiger* was a huge, four-engined Tudor IV owned by British-South American Airways. At 10.30 p.m. on the night of January 29, it radioed the control tower at Kindley Field, Bermuda, that it was 400 miles northeast of the island.

"'Weather and performance excellent,' the pilot reported. 'Expect to arrive on schedule.'

"That was the last message ever received from the airliner with its six crewmen and twenty-three passengers.

"At dawn a search was launched. The US Navy ordered ten surface vessels out. Over thirty military and civilian planes covered the region. There was no wreckage, no bodies, no oil slicks.

"Late on the following day bad weather set in, and by nightfall on the 31st the planes were recalled. The vessels continued their fruitless search for several more days.

"Later, in London, there was an official court of investigation. The court concluded that the *Star Tiger* was 'presumed lost at sea,' since there was no actual evidence, and that the mishap must have had 'some external cause.'"

And so it goes on. On December 28, 1948, a DC-3 passenger plane took off from San Juan, Puerto Rico, on route to Miami a thousand miles away. The thirty-two passengers, including two babies, had been spending the Christmas holidays on the island. By 4.13 a.m. the following morning, they were almost home. Captain

Linquist made his last contact with the Miami control tower. "We're approaching field," he said, "only fifty miles out to the south. All's well. Will stand by for landing instructions." That was the last anyone heard of the plane. It vanished – apparently into thin air.

Twenty days later, the Bermuda jinx struck again. On January 17, 1949, the *Ariel*, another four-engined Tudor IV took off from Bermuda at 7.45 a.m. for a four hour flight to Kingston, Jamaica. It's fuel tanks were full, and it had fuel for another ten hours of flight in its reserve tanks. At 8.25 a.m. Captain McPhee reported, "We are approximately 180 miles south of Bermuda. Weather fair. All is well. I'm changing radio frequency to pick up Kingston." That was the last that was ever heard of it.

And so the losses went on – of a Globemaster in 1950, of a British York transport plane in 1952, of a Navy Super Constellation in 1954, of another Martin C plane in 1956, of an Air Force tanker in 1962, of two Strato-tankers in 1963, of a flying boxcar in 1965, of a civilian cargo plane in 1966, another cargo plane in 1967, and yet another in 1973 . . . . the total number of lives lost in all these disappearances was well in excess of two hundred.

After publication of his article in *Argosy*, Gaddis received many letters from readers with suggested explanations. These included interference from flying saucers to space-warps that caused the planes and ships to enter another dimension. But one letter from a Mr Dick Stern of Atlanta, Georgia, told of an incident that seemed to throw a little light on the problem. Stern described how, during the last weeks of 1944, his bombing group left the United States for Italy, where they were to serve as reinforcements.

61

"Not more than 300 miles from Bermuda on a beautiful clear night, we were suddenly whipped over on our back, found ourselves on the ceiling one moment and pinned down the next, as the ship was thrown about at an incredible rate of speed. Our pilot was a 240-pound strong man, and our co-pilot was six-feet-one and 200 pounds of hard muscle. I watched them pulling on the wheels with all their combined strength to avert a sure crash into the ocean, only a few hundred feet below. They miraculously pulled out of the dive so close to the water that the wind-generated white caps were clearly visible.

"The entire incident took only a matter of seconds, perhaps less than one minute, but when we surveyed the crew, eleven frightened men had been reduced to quivering boys who unanimously agreed to resign from the Air Force.

"We headed back to Bermuda, and no sooner had we landed than we jumped from the plane, almost to a man, kissed the ground and announced to one and all that we were now solid infantry men. We were told that of the seven planes which had taken off in our 'box', only two had returned, and nothing was ever heard from the others. No wreckage was sighted, there had been no radio contact. And yet it was a clear starry night.

"We subsequently regained our composure after a few weeks in Bermuda, while the Air Force conducted a thorough, if somewhat futile, search and investigation.

"Three years ago, my wife and I were returning from London by plane via a route which took us to Bermuda, then to Nassau and on to Miami where we lived.

"After leaving Bermuda on what appeared to be a

clear day with only a thunderstorm playing on the distant horizon, I was discussing the area with the pilot and my wife was relating the above incident. At almost the same moment, we were thrown into a tremendous shock treatment that dropped the plane (a Bristol Britannia) with such force that the food we were eating was thrown to the ceiling. Fortunately, we had our seat belts fastened or we would have hit the ceiling in the same manner.

"After a harrowing fifteen minutes of up and down, and no storm in our immediate vicinity, we managed to clear the area."

John Gebhard was hanged in Cape Province Prison in November 1856 for the murder of a man called Pierre Villiers on a farm not far from Cape Town, South Africa. Villiers had been found strangled and his money and valuables were missing. One of the chief witnesses against Gebhard was a fellow farm laborer, Peter Lorenz.

Gebhard maintained his innocence to the end. As he stood on the scaffold, he told the priest, Father Dupre, "I am innocent. No grave will hold my body." Moments later, the trap dropped. Gebhard was buried on the slopes of Paarl Mountain.

Because many people believed in Gebhard's innocence, and the prison governor suspected that his last words meant that his body might be taken from its grave, the governor set a guard over the graveyard for the next two months.

Then, suddenly, Gebhard was proved innocent. The owner of the farm where Villiers had died found a purse belonging to the murder victim in the possession of Peter Lorenz, the man whose testimony had hanged Gebhard. Search of Lorenz's bunk revealed more of the dead man's possessions. The prison governor ordered that Gebhard's body should be exhumed and reburied in consecrated ground. Gebhard's mother was given a lump sum in compensation and a pension from the government. Mrs Gebhard was present when the coffin was removed from the grave. But when the lid was removed, it proved to be empty. Yet the governor swore that the grave had been constantly guarded for the past two months.

Gebhard's body was never found. But in August 1956, picnickers on the slopes of Paarl Mountain found a marble slab with an inscription, "Sacred to the memory of John Gebhard." It is now in the museum at Paarl, Cape Town. Since executed criminals were buried in unmarked graves, this is another mystery that has never been solved.

In his book *Invisible Horizons* (1965), Gaddis goes on to talk about the disappearance of vessels and ships in good condition found mysteriously abandoned in or near the triangle, and points out that this goes back for over a century. His records begin, he says, in 1840, when a large French ship called the *Rosalie*, bound for Havana, was found in or near the triangle. Most of her sails were set, cargo intact, everything shipshape, but the only living thing aboard was a half-starved canary in a cage.

The German ship *Freya* sailed from Manzanillo, Cuba, on October 3, 1902, for Chile. Seventeen days later she was found partly dismasted, listing badly and nobody aboard.

In April 1932, the Greek schooner *Embiricos*, while sailing fifty miles south of Bermuda, found the two-masted *John and Mary* of New York, her sails furled, the hull freshly painted, but no one aboard.

In February 1940, the yacht *Gloria Colita* of St Vincent, in the British West Indies, was found drifting in the Gulf of Mexico. Everything was in order. The sea was calm. But there was no one on board.

He goes on to mention other ships that have simply disappeared – the British frigate *Atalanta*, a training ship with 290 cadets and sailors aboard, which left Bermuda for England in January 1890 and vanished; the *USS Cyclops*, which sailed from Barbados, British West Indies, on March 4, 1918 with 309 people on board and simply vanished; in 1925, the cargo ship *SS Cotopaxi* vanished on the voyage from Charleston to Havana, and in 1926 the freighter *Suduffco* vanished after sailing south from Port Newark with a crew of 29 men.

Gaddis received another letter from a man who had survived the Bermuda Triangle. His name was Gerald Hawkes, and he described how (in April 1952), on a flight from Idlewild Airport (now Kennedy) to Bermuda, his plane had suddenly dropped about 200 feet. This was not a nose-dive but felt as if he had suddenly fallen down a lift shaft in the air; then the plane shot back up again. "It was as if a giant hand was holding the plane and jerking it up and down," and the wings seemed to flap like the wings of a bird. The captain then told them that he was unable to find Bermuda, and that the operator was unable to make radio contact with either the US or Bermuda. An hour or so later the plane made contact with a radio ship, and was able to get its bearings and fly to Bermuda. As they climbed out of the plane they observed that it was a clear and starry night with no wind. The writer concluded that he was still wondering whether he was caught in an area "where time and space seemed to disappear."

Of course, planes caught in air pockets or violent air turbulence are not unusual, but the total radio blackout also seems typical of the mystery of the Bermuda Triangle.

Gaddis's book caused a great deal of speculation – much of it about the possibility that flying saucers or aliens from space were responsible for the disappearances. Someone produced the interesting theory that perhaps alien intelligences knew about the strange mystery-vortex in the area of Bermuda and was using it to collect human specimens. A friend of Vincent Gaddis, Ivan Sanderson, a zoologist, felt that this was going too far. He began by taking a map of the world and marking on it a number of areas where strange disappearances had occurred. There was, for example, another "devil's triangle" south of the Japanese island of Honshu where ships and planes had vanished. A correspondent told Sanderson about a strange experience on a flight to Guam, in the western pacific, when his ancient propeller-driven plane covered 340 miles in one hour, although there was no wind – about 200 miles more than it should have covered; checks showed that many planes had vanished in this area. Marking such areas on the map, Sanderson observed that they were shaped like lozenges, and that these lozenges seem to ring the globe in a neat symmetry, running in two circles, each between 30 degrees and 40 degrees north and south of the Equator. There were ten of these "funny places", about 72 degrees apart. An earthquake specialist named George Rouse had argued that earthquakes originated in a certain layer below the earth's surface, and had speculated that there was a kind of trough running round the central core of the earth, which determined the direction of seismic activities. Rouse's map of these siesmic disturbance areas corresponded closely with Sanderson's "lozenges." So Sanderson was inclined to believe that if "whirlpools" really cause the disappearance of ships and planes, then they were perfectly normal physical whirlpools, caused, so to speak, by the earth's tendency to "burp."

Sanderson's *Invisible Residents* (1970), subtitled *Startling evidence for the possibility of intelligent life under water by a distinguished naturalist and scientist*, included his chapter on the Bermuda Triangle and the "lozenges" spread around the world like a belt, and suggests that perhaps the answer lies in "magnetic vortices", some kind of strange anomaly in the earth's magnetic field which occurs in regular sequence around the equator.

In 1973, the first book on the Bermuda Triangle (by a writer called Adi-Kent Thomas Jeffrey), came out in America. Unfortunately, it was only eighty-six pages long, and was published by a small publisher in New Hope, Pennsylvania. It was unfortunate that she failed to interest some major New York publisher in her book. Although short, it is an excellent piece of work and would undoubtedly have reached the bestseller lists, as Berlitz's would do a year later. It must be admitted that Ms Jeffrey is an excellent story teller. She describes how Bermuda was found by the Spanish explorer Juan de

Bermudez in 1515, and that no one felt any interest in the place. It remained unoccupied for almost a century. Then, in July 1609, a ship called the *Sea Venture* was taking settlers to the new founded colony of Virginia. As they came close to Bermuda they were hit by a tremendous storm, and seas that raised the ship high in the air and then plunged it down into watery valleys. The expedition leader, Sir George Somers, kept his men pumping and bailing for four days. Finally, just as he felt there was no further hope, he sighted Bermuda and managed to land the ship in a wedge-shaped reef. There, the 150 passengers managed to land and to take all the necessary equipment ashore before another tremendous sea sucked the ship out of the wedge of the reef and sank it.

The passengers found life on Bermuda less uncomfortable than they had feared. There was plenty of wood to build themselves shelters, and plenty of fish, lobsters, crabs and turtles in the sea. From the beginning, Bermuda was a holiday island. In fact, when he heard about it, William Shakespeare decided to use it in his latest play, *The Tempest*, in which the wreck of the *Sea Venture* is immortalised. But Somers' description of the tremendous storm that almost destroyed them makes us aware that the dangers of the Bermuda Triangle are not all as mysterious as we might suppose.

Shortly after that occurred the first mysterious vanishing in the Bermuda Triangle. A month after the wreck of the *Sea Venture* on August 28, 1609, the long boat of the ship set out under the command of the mate, Henry Ravens, to try and bring rescue. It was a sturdy craft, and a stout canvas sail promised to carry it safely to land. Two nights later, the long boat returned and Ravens explained that he had been unable to escape from the reefs around the island.

On September 1, the long boat set out again. Ravens was accompanied by seven men, and there was a good supply of food and water on board. Nevertheless, the long boat was never seen again.

For another eight months, the castaways lived on their desert island, and managed to built two seaworthy boats. They left Bermuda on May 10, 1610, and arrived in Jamestown, Virginia (580 miles away) two weeks later. They hoped to hear news of the missing long boat but that had vanished for ever.

In 1750, five Spanish galleons, under the command of Captain Don Juan Manuel de Bonilla set out to sail from Havana, Cuba, to Spain. They were struck by a tremendous hurricane and the captain was forced to lash himself to the wheel. Four strong sailors had to help him to try and hold it. In spite of the pumps, the ships began to sink. The captain ordered the carpenters to cut away the lanyards and a tremendous wave immediately carried them away. The main mast splintered and crashed down on the deck. The galleon almost overturned but slowly righted herself. By the following day at dawn, it was able to find shelter in the mouth of the Ocracoke River. But of the other four galleons there was no sign. One of them, he learned later, had been wrecked near Norfolk, Virginia.

Fortunately for Bonilla, England and Spain had only just signed a treaty ending a long period of hostility, and Bonilla was a guest of Governor Johnston of the Carolina colony until he sailed back to Spain. Nothing of the other three galleons was ever found.

Adi-Kent Thomas Jeffrey ends her book by telling the

story of Flight 19, and then goes on to discuss briefly the "Devil's Triangle" off Japan, pointing out that its seas are made dangerous because of the eruptions of the Fuji Volcano.

In the following year, Charles Berlitz in *The Bermuda Triangle* suddenly managed to make the whole world aware of the mystery. The book sold five billion copies in various languages. Berlitz is the grandson of the man who founded the famous language schools, and he simply rehashed all the information about the Bermuda Triangle and persuaded a commercial publisher, Doubleday, to issue it. The book, which is highly readable, is low on scholarly precision – it does not even have an index. One reason for its popularity was that he launched himself intrepidly into bizarre regions of speculation about UFOs, space-time warps, alien intelligences, Chariots of the Gods (à la von Daniken) and other such matters. The weirdest of his speculations were those concerning the pioneer "ufologist" Morris K. Jessup, who had died in strange circumstances after stumbling upon information about a certain mysterious "Philadelphia experiment." This experiment was supposed to have taken place in Philadelphia in 1943, when the Navy was testing some new device whose purpose was to surround a ship with a powerful magnetic field. According to Jessup's informant, a hazy green light began to surround the vessel, so that its outlines became blurred; then it vanished – to reappear in the harbour of Norfolk, Virginia, some 300 miles away. Several members of the crew died, others went insane. According to Jessup, when he began to investigate this story, the navy asked him whether he would be willing to work on a similar secret project and he declined. In 1959 he was found dead in his car, suffocated by exhaust gas. The obvious explanation is suicide in a state of depression – but Berlitz speculates that he was "silenced" before he could publicize his discoveries about the experiment.

The Philadelphia experiment, of course, was supposed to be an attempt to create a "magnetic vortex" like those suggested by Sanderson. According to Jessup, it had the effect of involving the ship in a space-time warp that transported it hundreds of miles. Although the story sounds preposterous, there are still a number of people who insist that it is true. In fact, two of these people – Al Bielek and Duncan Cameron – insist that they were actually involved in the original experiment. This, they say, took place on a test ship called the *USS Eldridj* in 1943, at the Philadelphia Navy Yard. The aim was not to make anyone invisible, but simply to surround the ship with a kind of magnetic field that would make it undetectable to radar. Some extremely distinguished persons were alleged to be involved – the brilliant scientist Nicola Tesla, the mathematician John von Neumann and the psychologist Wilhelm Reich. The tests they were involved in were known as Project Rainbow. The aim was to create a kind of "magnetic bottle" around the ship. Realising that the project was dangerous, Tesla is said to have sabotaged the first scheduled experiment with a live crew because he wanted more time for research – and as a consequence was dismissed from the project in 1942. He died in the following year. Tesla's second in command, John von Neumann (inventor of games theory and the great computer pioneer) took over from Tesla. Cameron

71

and Bielek claimed that they were control-room officers. According to Bielek and Cameron, the initial experiment was carried out on July 20, 1943, when the generators were turned on for fifteen minutes. The ship not only disappeared from radar but also became invisible. The crew on deck experienced nausea and disorientation. But Bielek and Cameron, in the control-room, experienced no ill effects.

In spite of Neumann's pleas for delay, a second experiment was carried out on August 12, 1943. Bielek claims that three UFOs appeared over the ship six days before the test. Once again, the *Eldridj* apparently disappeared. When Bielek and Cameron came out on deck, they discovered that nothing was visible around the ship and that most of the crew were either insane or dead. These included, according to Duncan Cameron, one of his brothers. Cameron and Beilek tried to swim away from the ship. It reappeared four hours later and most of the crew were given discharges on grounds of being mentally unfit. According to Bielek, he and Cameron were "brainwashed" using a technique which is ascribed to Wilhelm Reich, the great sexual psychologist who claimed to have discovered an invisible universal energy called orgone energy.

The work of Project Rainbow was later continued at Montauk on Long Island, where it attracted the attention of a man called Preston B. Nichols, who was working for a defence contractor on Long Island. He became interested in a technique that Reich is alleged to have developed – an instrument for controlling the weather which involved a simple radio broadcasting device. And when Nichols – who supplemented his income by buying up second-hand radio equipment and reselling it – bought a great deal of Wilhelm Reich's own radio equipment for a few hundred dollars, he discovered that he also had a box full of Reich's files and notebooks. Readers who are interested in following up this strange and extremely complicated story are recommended to Nichols's book *The Montauk Project – Experiments in Time* (1992).

With such extraordinary tales, it is not surprising that Berlitz's book achieved bestsellerdom. But the nearest he comes to explaining the mystery of the Bermuda Triangle is when he quotes the experience of Captain Don Henry in 1966. Henry was the owner of a salvage company in Miami, Florida, called The Phantom Exploration Company. He states, "We were coming in on the return trip between Puerto Rico and Fort Lauderdale. We had been out for three days towing an empty barge . . . . I was aboard the *Good News*, a 160-foot-long tug of 2,000 horsepower . . . .

"It was afternoon, the weather was good and the sky was clear. I had gone to the cabin in back of the bridge for a few minutes when I heard a lot of hollering going on. I came out of the cabin on to the bridge and yelled 'What the hell is going on?' The first thing I looked at was the compass, which was spinning clockwise. There was no reason that this should ever happen – the only place beside here I ever heard it to happen was in the St Lawrence River at Kingston, where a big deposit of iron or maybe a meteorite on the bottom makes the compasses go crazy. I did not know what had happened, but something big was sure as hell going on. The water seemed to be coming from all directions. The horizon disappeared – we couldn't see where the horizon was – the water, sky, and all the horizon were

73

blended together. We couldn't see where we were.

"Whatever was happening robbed, stole or borrowed everything from our generators. All electric appliances and outlets ceased to produce power. The generators were still running, but we weren't getting any power. The engineer tried to start an auxiliary generator but couldn't get a spark . . . . I rammed the throttles full ahead. I couldn't see where we were going, but I wanted to get the hell out in a hurry. It seemed that something wanted to pull us back, but couldn't quite make it.

"Coming out of it was like coming out of a fog bank. When we came out, the tow-line was sticking out straight – like the Indian rope trick – with nothing visible at the end of it where it was covered by a fog concentrated around it. I jumped to the main deck and pulled. The damned barge came out from the fog, but there was no fog any place else. In fact I could see for eleven miles. In the foggy area where the tow should have been, the water was confused although the waves were not big . . . .

"Have you ever felt two people pulling on your arms in opposite directions? I felt that we were on a place or point that somebody or something wanted, and somebody or something wanted us to be in another place from where we were going."

Asked if there was a greenish appearance to the horizon, he replied, "No, it was milky. That's all I can say. I wasn't looking for colors. After we left, the batteries had to be recharged. I had to throw away fifty flashlight batteries."

So, according to Henry, whatever force caused his problems was able to drain the batteries of energy and to cause the compass to go awry. Many people who have seen UFOs have reported that the car suddenly stopped and that nothing they could do would get it started again. But in these cases, the power disappeared completely. The electrical force of the Bermuda Triangle seems to leave the power running.

The following case is reported in the *Journal of the Society For Psychical Research* for 1942.

In early June 1933, Mr and Mrs Clifford H. Pye were staying at Falmouth on the south coast of Cornwall. It was very hot and after ten days they decided to move to north Cornwall. They took a train from Falmouth to Wadebridge, and then took a bus past Camelford and Tintagel to Boscastle. Approaching Boscastle, they both began to look out for a hotel or guest house. Just before reaching the steep hairpin bend which drops downhill into the town, the bus stopped to set down a passenger and they saw a guest house on the left hand side of the road. It had a semi-circular drive, with a gate at either end. Clifford Pye describes it as looking as if it had been built in the 1860s or early 1870s, with a fresh, trim appearance and a lawn with scarlet geraniums and tables shaded by large garden umbrellas coloured in black and orange.

A few minutes later, Mr and Mrs Pye were set down in Boscastle. It was a hot day and they disliked the smell of the seaweed in the sun. So they decided not to look for a guest house in the town, but to go back to the one they had seen at the top of the hill. While Clifford Pye stayed to guard the luggage, his wife walked back up the hill to try and book them a room.

Clifford Pye became increasingly anxious as almost an hour-and-a-half went by. Finally his wife returned, looking

---

worried and hot. She said that she had simply been unable to find the house at the top of the hill and had walked further on until she got to a village called Trevalga, a mile-and-a-half away, where she had booked rooms.

Her husband was equally puzzled, and on the bus that took them back from Boscastle to Trevalga, he sat on the right hand side and peered out of the window for any sign of the house. "It's just here, about fifty yards further on," he said to his wife. But there was no house fifty yards further on – just empty fields. They were so puzzled that they made a thorough investigation of the area during their time at Trevalga and described the house to a number of people – all of whom assured them that it did not exist.

The eminent psychical investigator Sir Ernest Bennett came to hear of the case, and persuaded both Mr and Mrs Pye to write a full account of their experience. Both of them told exactly the same story of the disappearing house. The only discrepancy between their two accounts was that Mrs Pye thought the house was slightly further from Boscastle than her husband did. But that made no difference, since there was no such house anyway.

A pilot named Chuck Wakeley also had a strange story to tell. "In November of 1964 I was a pilot for Sunline Aviation in Miami. During this time I took a charter flight to Nassau to drop off some people and return. I dropped off the passengers and left Nassau Airport shortly after dark. The weather was very clear and the stars were shining . . . . I had levelled off at about 8,000 feet and was settling back for a routine flight but, thirty to fifty miles past Andros, on a direct heading for Bimini, I began to notice something unusual – a very faint glowing effect on the wings. At first I thought it was an illusion created by the cockpit lights shining through the tinted Plexiglas window . . . . in the course of about five minutes this glow increased in intensity until it became so bright that I had great difficulty reading my instruments. My magnetic compass began revolving, slowly but steadily; the fuel gauges, which had read 'half full' at takeoff, now read 'full.' My electric autopilot suddenly put the aircraft into a hard right turn, and I had to shut it off and operate manually. I could not trust any of the electrically run instruments, as they were either totally out or behaving erratically. Soon the whole aircraft was glowing, but it was not a reflected glow, since the glow was coming from the aircraft itself. When I looked out of the window at the wings I remembered noticing that they were not only glowing bluish-green, but also looked fuzzy . . . . I did the only thing I could – that was to let go of the controls, and let the craft fly on whatever heading it would take. The glow built up to a blinding crescendo of light, lasted for about five minutes, and then diminished gradually.

"All instruments began to function normally as soon as the glowing dissipated. I checked all circuit breakers and none had popped. No fuses were blown and I realised that the equipment was functioning normally when the fuel gauges returned to reading that the tanks were 'half full.' The magnetic compass became steady and showed that I was only a few degrees off course. I engaged the autopilot and it was normal."

It seems, then, highly likely that there is some

unknown electrical force in the Bermuda Triangle which causes problems to modern electrical equipment. It may or may not be relevant that in 1609, when the *Sea Venture* was wrecked on Bermuda, the captain, Sir George Somers described in his log how, soon after the ship entered what is now called the Bermuda Triangle, there was a remarkable display of phantom lights around the masts – the phenomenon known as St Elmo's fire, an electrical discharge caused by the friction between the masts of the ship – or an aeroplane – and the surrounding air.

Although it seems clear that there *is* some strange force operating in the area of the Bermuda Triangle, it would be unwise to allow this to blind us entirely to more natural explanations. Lawrence David Kusche made the admirable decision to study all the basic official documents about the Bermuda Triangle. He published these in his book *The Bermuda Triangle Mystery – Solved*, which is certainly required reading for anybody interested in the Triangle. His account of the disappearance of Flight 19 deserves to be studied with care. It runs to twenty-one pages, and quotes extensively from the Navy investigation report, which is more than four hundred pages long. Kusche begins by making the point that all the crew members, with the exception of Taylor, were trainee pilots. And Taylor himself was a newcomer to the base and was unfamiliar with the area. The original account as given by Gaddis states that the Martin-Mariner search plane took off soon after Flight 19 lost radio contact, 4.30 p.m. In fact, it took off three hours later. It was heard to explode approximately twenty minutes after take off, "exactly where airplane should have been after twenty-three minutes of flight." Mariners were nicknamed "flying gastanks" because of the fumes (of gasoline) which were often present, and a crewman sneaking a cigarette or a spark from any source could have caused the explosion.

The Mariner was not the only search plane. It was not even the first to take off. The Dinner Key (Miami) Dumbo was in the air at 6.20 p.m., but its antenna quickly iced over and it was unable to communicate. Search planes left Vero Beach at 6.45 p.m. and Daytona Beach at 7.21 p.m. Training 32 and 49 did not leave Banana River until about 7.30 p.m. Other planes took off later still, and a number of ships were also sent to the scene.

Kusche comments that Taylor's unfamiliarity with the Bahamas "could account for his erroneous assumption that he was over the Florida Keys. Taylor could not decide whether he was over the Atlantic Ocean and east of Florida, or over the Gulf of Mexico and west of the peninsula. As a result he changed direction a number of times, led the men back and forth, and progressively moved further north of the Bahamas." Taylor also failed to change his radio to the emergency channel, afraid that he might lose touch with the other planes in his flight who might not be able to change to the emergency channel. It seems clear that, having first mistaken his position, Taylor lost his nerve. Kusche says "the use of the emergency channel would also have permitted the direction-finding stations to have found the flight position much earlier."

The main problem was the very bad weather. "The dilemma was not that the men couldn't tell in which direction they were going, but rather that they couldn't decide which direction was the proper one to take. They weren't sure which side of the Florida peninsula they were on, and continually changed direction, usually taking a heading of east or west. Another time they flew north, as Taylor said, to be sure they were not over the Gulf of Mexico." Kusche says, "It has frequently been said that it is inconceivable that the airplanes could have vanished in such a restricted area. According to the official report, however, they flew around lost, for more than four hours before finally running out of fuel. They went down in the Atlantic Ocean somewhere east of the United States and north of the Bahamas."

Many factors, Kusche says, prevented Flight 19 from being saved – the failure of Lieutenant Taylor's compasses, failure of the one radio channel needed to continue communication with the flight, bad radio reception, the delay in sending out rescue planes, the approach of night and the invasion of bad weather, the inability to locate the flight promptly with radio bearings, the failure to broadcast the position of fix once it was known, the failure of the teletype system, the icing of the Dinner Key Dumbo's antenna, the military discipline that kept the group together even though several of the pilots knew they were headed the wrong way. Kusche concludes, "The most tragic part of the incident is that when Lieutenant Taylor first reported his predicament, he was, according to later testimony, over the reefs and keys just north of the Bahamas. Flight 19 was almost exactly on course when the pilots decided they were lost!"

All this, of course, still does not explain why the compasses suddenly went wrong.

In most of the cases discussed in the book, Kusche is excellent in suggesting common sense reasons for what went wrong. For example, when, in March 1948, Al Snider (a famous jockey) disappeared on a fishing trip near Sandy Key, Kusche points out that an enormous storm blew up and that the three men in a small rowboat had gone off fishing in the dark. All the same, there are many cases where Kusche admits that he has no explanation. For example, after a long analysis of the disappearance of the *Star Tiger* in January 1968, Kusche ends by admitting, "The disappearance of the *Star Tiger* thwarts all explanation as each of the suggested solutions seems too unlikely to have occurred. It is truly a modern mystery of the air." It seems, then, that in spite of all the attempts to debunk the "legend", the Bermuda Triangle remains one of the greatest mysteries of our time.

It is important to realise that the earth is a giant magnet, but that its magnetism is not as uniform as that of an ordinary bar magnet. The magnetic lines of force that run around its surface have strange patterns. Birds and animals use these lines of force for "homing", and water diviners seem to be able to respond to them with their "dowsing rods." But there are areas of the earth's surface where birds lose their way because the lines somehow cancel one another out, forming a magnetic anomaly or vortex. The *Marine Observer* for 1930 warns sailors about a magnetic disturbance in the neighborhood of the Tambora Volcano, near Sumbawa, which deflected a ship's compass by six points, leading it off course. In 1932, Captain Scott of the *Australia* observed a magnetic disturbance near Freemantle that deflected the compass twelve degrees either side of the ship's course. Dozens of similar anomalies have been collected and documented by an American investigator, William Corliss, in books with titles like *Unknown Earth* and *Strange Planet*. It was Corliss who pointed out to me the investigations of Doctor John de Laurier of Ottawa, who in 1974 went to camp on the ice floes of northern Canada, in search of an enormous magnetic anomaly, 43 miles long which he believed to originate about eighteen miles below the surface of the earth. De Laurier's theory is that such anomalies are due to the earth's tectonic plates rubbing together – an occurrence that also causes earthquakes.

Scientists are not sure why the earth has a magnetic field but one theory suggests that it is due to movements in its molten iron core. Such movements would in fact produce shifting patterns in the earth's field, and bursts of magnetic activity, which might be compared to the bursts of solar energy known as sun spots. If they *are* related to earth-tensions, and therefore to earthquakes, then we would expect them to occur in certain definite zones, just as earthquakes do. What effects would a sudden "earthquake" of magnetic activity produce? One would be to cause compasses to spin, for it would be rather as if a huge magnetic meteor was roaring up from the center of the earth. On the sea it would produce an effect of violent turbulence, for it would affect the water in the same way the moon affects the tides but in an irregular pattern, so that the water would appear to be coming "from all directions." Clouds of mist would be sucked into the vortex forming a "bank" in its immediate area and electronic gadgetry would probably be put out of action . . . . all this makes us aware why the "simplicity" explanations of some of the books that try to dismiss the mystery of the Bermuda Triangle are not only superficial but dangerous. They discourage the investigation of what could be one of the most interesting scientific enigmas of our time. With satellites circling the earth at a height of 150 miles, it should be possible to observe bursts of magnetic activity with the same accuracy that earth tremors are recorded on seismographs. We should be able to observe their frequency and their intensity precisely enough to plot them in advance. The result could not only be the solution of the mystery, but the prevention of further tragedies like that of Flight 19.

4

Semi-Mysteries?

*In April 1915, allied armies landed on the Gallipoli Penin-
sula in European Turkey in an attempt to capture what is
now Istanbul, the capital of the Turkish Empire. They
wanted to make contact with Russian allies through the
Black Sea. It was a bad strategy. The Turkish resistance was
stubborn and the allies were forced to withdraw nine months
later, having lost hundreds of thousands of men.*

Never seen again

Some of the bloodiest fighting in Gallipoli took place
around a spot called "Hill 60" near Suvla Bay. On the
morning of August 28, 1915, a British regiment – the
First-Fourth Norfolk – prepared to attack "Hill 60". The
regiment consisted of more than a thousand men. It
was a warm, clear day, but several observers remember
noticing a group of curious low clouds over "Hill 60."
Although there was a breeze, these clouds seemed to
remain stationary. The observers reported watching the
regiment march uphill until the entire file of men
disappeared into one of these "loaf-shaped" clouds.
Then the clouds moved away – leaving no sign of the
army.

The disappearance of the regiment was reported to the British Government by the Commander-in-Chief of the allied expeditionary force in Gallipoli. He made no mention of the mysterious clouds, but reported that the regiment had separated from the main body of troops and had vanished. The whole regiment was subsequently posted as "missing" – the assumption being that all its men had been killed or taken prisoner. When the war ended in 1918, the British asked the Turks about their missing regiment. The Turks replied that they knew nothing about it. Their armies had never made contact with the First-Fourth Norfolk.

Fifty years later, at a reunion of an ANZAC (Australian and New Zealand Army Corps) regiment, three witnesses of the disappearance signed the following deposition:

August 21, 1915.

"The following is an account of the strange incident that happened on the above date, which occurred in the morning during the severest and final period of fighting which took place on "Hill 60", Suvla Bay, ANZAC.

"The day broke clear, without a cloud in sight, as any beautiful Mediterranean day could be expected to be. The exception, however, was a number of perhaps six or eight "loaf of bread" shaped clouds – all shaped exactly alike – which were hovering over "Hill 60". It was noticed that, in spite of a four or five-mile-an-hour breeze from the south, these clouds did not alter their position in any shape or form, nor did they drift away under the influence of the breeze. They were hovering at an elevation of about sixty degrees, as seen from our observation point five hundred feet up. Also stationary and resting on the ground right underneath this group of clouds was a similar cloud in shape, measuring about 800 feet in length, 220 feet in height, and 200 feet in width. This cloud was absolutely dense, solid looking in structure and positioned about fourteen to eighteen chains from the fighting in British-held territory. All this was observed by twenty-two men of number three section, number one field company, NZE, including myself, from our trenches on Rhododendron Spur, approximately 2,500 yards southwest of the cloud on the ground. Our vantage point was overlooking "Hill 60" by about 300 feet. As it turned out later, this singular cloud was straddling a dry creek bed or sunken road (Kaiajik Dere) and we had a perfect view of the cloud's sides and ends as it rested on the ground. Its color was a light grey, as was the color of the other clouds.

"A British regiment, the First-Fourth Norfolk, of several hundred men, was then noticed marching up this sunken road or creek towards "Hill 60". However, when they arrived at this cloud, they marched straight into it with no hesitation, but no one ever came out to deploy and fight at "Hill 60." About an hour later, after the last of the file had disappeared into it, this cloud very unobtrusively lifted off the ground and, like any cloud or fog would, rose slowly until it joined the other similar clouds which were mentioned at the beginning of this account. On viewing them again, they all looked alike "as peas in a pod." All this time, the group of clouds had been hovering in the same place, but as soon as the singular cloud had risen to their level, they all moved away northwards, i.e., towards Thrace (Bulgaria). In a matter of about three quarters of an hour

General Sir Ian Hamilton

they had all disappeared from view. The regiment mentioned was posted as missing or "wiped out" and on Turkey surrendering in 1918, the first thing Britain demanded of Turkey was the return of this regiment. Turkey replied that she had neither captured this regiment, nor made any contact with it, and did not know it existed. A British regiment in 1914–1918 consisted of any number between 800 and 4,000 men. Those who observed this incident vouch for the fact that Turkey never captured that regiment, nor made contact with it.

"We, the undersigned, although late in time, this is the fiftieth jubilee of the ANZAC landing, declare that the above described incident is true in every word.

"Signed by the witnesses:

"4/165 Sapper F. Reichardt, Matata Bay of Plenty.

"13/416 Sapper R. Newnes, 157 King Street, Cambridge.

"J. L. Newman, 75 Freyberg Street, Octumoctai, Tauranga.

It is not surprising then that many books on mysterious disappearances have cited this case as one that has been well authenticated.

This account contains one or two minor inaccuracies – the Norfolks who disappeared were the First-Fifth Battalion, only part of the First-Fourth Norfolk Regiment, and they disappeared on August 12, not August 21 – presumably someone typed the figures the wrong way round.

What of more official reports?

From a Final Report of the Dardanelles Commission, we know that the Commander-in-Chief, Sir Ian

Hamilton, had decided to stage a major attack on Turkish positions under cover of darkness on August 12–13. But at 4.00 p.m that afternoon, the attack was launched by the 163rd Brigade, with the First-Fourth Norfolk in the rear. Hamilton would have done better to stick to his original plan of launching the attack by night – the Turks had a clear view of the enemy, and wiped them out by the dozen.

Later, Sir Ian Hamilton sent a dispatch to Lord Kitchener, the Secretary of State for War:

"In the course of the fight, creditable in all respects of the 163rd Brigade, there happened a very mysterious thing . . . . against the yielding forces of the enemy, Colonel Sir H. Beauchamp, a bold, self-confident officer, eagerly pressed forward, followed by the best part of the battalion. The fighting grew hotter, and the ground became more wooded and broken. At this stage many men were wounded or grew exhausted with thirst. These found their way back to camp during the night. But the Colonel, with 16 officers and 250 men, still kept pushing forward, driving the enemy before him . . . . nothing more was seen or heard of any of them. They charged into the forest and were lost to sight or sound. Not one of them ever came back."

So it looks as if this disappearance of the Colonel and 250 men was the basis of the story of the disappearing regiment. Eventually, after losing 46,000 men, the British decided to withdraw at the end of 1915. The Dardanelles campaign had been a disaster. But the Turks were defeated – partly with the help of Lawrence of Arabia and his Arab forces – and when the British came back to Gallipoli in 1918, it was as an occupying force. There, on the battlefield of Gallipoli, someone found a cap badge of the Royal Norfolk Regiment, and was told that a Turkish farmer had dumped a large number of bodies of British soldiers in a nearby ravine. The bodies were recovered, and on September 23, 1919, the Graves Registration Unit announced:

"We have found the Fifth Norfolk – there were 180 in all: 122 Norfolk and a few Hants and Suffolks with 2/4th Cheshires. We could only identify two – Privates Barnaby and Carter. They were scattered over an area of one square mile, at a distance of at least 800 yards behind the Turkish front line. Many of them had evidently been killed in a farm, as a local Turk, who owns the land, told us that when he came back he found the farm covered with the decomposing bodies of British soldiers, which he threw into a small ravine. The whole thing quite bears out the original theory that they did not go very far on, but got mopped up one by one, all except the ones who got into the farmhouse."

So, gradually, the First-Fourth Norfolk is reduced from 1,000 men to 250 men – as reported by Sir Ian Hamilton – and finally to 122 men. That, as Paul Begg points out in his account in *Into Thin Air*, still leaves more than half of the Norfolks unaccounted for. But (as he points out), with slaughter on such an enormous scale, 128 men could easily vanish. Of course, there remains the account of the ANZACs, with its precise description of the men disappearing into a "loaf-shaped" cloud. In fact, there *were* extremely heavy clouds on August 21, nine days after the so-called disappearance of the First-Fourth Norfolks. This covered the whole battleground in fog, and made attack practically impossible. It may well be that the

ANZACs were simply confusing the two dates.

In all probability, the same close examination would solve the secret of another example of a disappearing regiment. In December 1937, China and Japan had been at war for six months, and the Chinese were getting the worse of the struggle. Shanghai fell and in spite of the protests of the League of Nations, the Japanese advanced on the capital Nanking.

South of the city, the Chinese commander, Colonel Li Fu Sien, decided to make a last-ditch stand in the low hills. An urgent request brought over 3,000 reinforcements. The colonel disposed these troops in a two-mile line close to an important bridge across the Yangtze River. They had a quantity of heavy artillery, and were prepared for a life-and-death struggle. The colonel returned to his headquarters a mile behind the lines, and waited for the Japanese attack. At dawn he was awakened by his aide who told him they were unable to contact the army. Had they been overrun by the Japanese in the night? The colonel and an escort drove cautiously towards the right flank to investigate. To their amazement, the positions were deserted. The guns were still in position – but the men had vanished. Further investigation revealed that a small pocket of soldiers, about 100, were still encamped near the bridge. They had heard no sounds in the night. If the army had deserted or surrendered to the Japanese, they would have had to pass close to the camp. The sentries on the bridge also testified that no one had crossed the bridge in the night. 3,000 men cannot vanish into thin air. Even if they had all deserted, such a mass exodus would have been bound to attract attention. Yet no one had heard or seen anything.

Lawrence of Arabia

The Chinese had little time to ponder the problem. The Japanese advanced across the river, and two days later Nanking fell. There followed one of the most horrifying and cruel massacres in history – the "rape" of Nanking. The atrocities were so appalling that three Japanese commanders were recalled to Japan, as were many soldiers. The "vanishing army" ceased to be a matter of central importance to the Chinese generals. But it was generally expected that the mystery would be solved when peace returned – that perhaps the solution lay in the records of the Japanese army. In fact the Japanese army reports contained no mention of the missing 3,000 men. Today they are regarded as the mysterious casualties of war. But no one knows what became of them.

Again, the story has been told repeatedly. But in this case, the Japanese remained the victors until their defeat at the end of World War II. And since the Japanese advanced the next day, and everything turned into the confusion of retreat, it seems highly probable that (like the First-Fourth Regiment of Norfolks), the missing army simply changed its position during the night, and the Chinese had no time to search for them thoroughly the next day. What happens, clearly, is that a story has a certain amount of foundation, and may even appear in official reports – like the First-Fourth Norfolk – but the memory is exaggerated by the survivors, and small details are added to make the whole thing more mysterious than, in fact, it was.

Strange Disappearances

This also applies to the greatest sea mystery of all time, the *Mary Celeste*.

In July 1882, a 23-year-old newly qualified doctor moved to Southsea, a suburb of Portsmouth, and screwed up his name plate. He had no definite plans for the future. He rented a house for forty pounds a year, then sat back to wait for patients. For many weeks none appeared, so he whiled away the time writing stories. In fact, he'd already had a few published – at about three guineas each (£3.15) – and many more rejected. His penchant was for tales of bizarre adventure set in Africa or the Arctic (he had visited both places as a ship's doctor); his style was influenced by Brett Hart (the chronicler of California's mining camps), and had a touch of facetiousness.

Some time that autumn, he began a story: "In the month of December 1873, the British ship *Dei Gratia* steered into Gibraltar, having in tow a derelict brigantine *Marie Celeste*, which it had picked up in latitude 38 40, longitude 17 15W." For such a short sentence, this contains a remarkable number of inaccuracies. The year was actually 1872; the *Dei Gratia* did not tow the *Marie Celeste*, the latter came under its own sail; the latitude and longitude are wrong; and the ship was called plain Mary, not Marie. All the same, when "J. Habakuk Jephson's Statement" was published in the *Cornhill Magazine* in 1884 it caused a sensation, launching Doctor Arthur Doyle's career as a writer – he was soon using the name A. Conan Doyle.

The J. Habakuk Jephson of the title is a doctor who specialises in tuberculosis. Wounded during the American Civil War, Jephson is nursed back to health on a southern plantation, where an old negress presents him with a curious black stone in the shape of a human ear.

Later, he himself contracts consumption, and decides that he needs a sea voyage. He becomes a passenger on the *Marie Celeste*. Several of the crew are negroes, and one of Jephson's fellow passengers is a quadroon (one-quarter negro) called Septimius Goring, from New Orleans. The captain is called Tibbs, and his wife and baby are also on board. After only a few days at sea, the captain's wife and child disappear. It is obvious that they have fallen overboard. A few days later, the distraught captain dies with a bullet through the head, apparently a suicide.

While Jephson is showing one of his passengers the black stone, one of the negro crewmen happens to see it, and is obviously deeply impressed. Goring asks if he can show it to the black steersman, and comes back a few moments later saying that it is worthless. He is about to throw it overboard when one of the black men catches his hand and makes him give it back.

The compass then goes wrong, and to their astonishment, the crew find themselves off the coast of Africa. At this point, a canoe full of negroes comes alongside and they take over the ship, tying everybody up. Goring, it turns out, is the ringleader of this coup. He is apparently a kind of Black Power leader who hates the white race and has committed a whole series of unsolved murders of whites over the past few years. He now tells Jephson that he is being forced to spare his life, because of their reverence to the ear-shaped stone.

Everyone else on the ship is murdered. But Jephson is taken ashore to a small town, in the centre of which is a kind of black idol which has one ear missing. Jephson's stone proves to be the missing ear. He learns that the inhabitants of the town are Mohammedans, and that the black statue is actually a large piece of the original black meteorite housed in the Kaaba in Mecca. The ear was taken by a breakaway sect and ended up in America.

The black meteorite at Kaaba

Goring helps Jephson to escape – not out of goodwill, but simply because he wants to become leader of the sect and the reverence in which the natives hold Jephson is an obstacle. And so Jephson is placed in a sailboat with food and water, and he eventually reaches the canaries. Now that he knows he is dying, he finally tells his story.

When "J. Habakuk Jephson's Statement" appeared in *The Cornhill*, it caused a sensation. It was published anonymously, and so gave the impression that it was actually by J. Habakuk Jephson. Understandably, most people took it for the truth and from then on it was widely accepted that the *Mary Celeste* had been taken over by a kind of Black Power leader with a hatred of whites. Mr Solly Flood, the chief investigator in the *Mary Celeste*, was so indignant at the inaccuracies of the story that he sent a telegram to the Central News Agency denouncing J. Habukuk Jephson as a fraud and a liar. The ensuing publicity made Conan Doyle's reputation, and from then on the *Cornhill* was willing to publish anything he wrote.

According to Doyle's story, the *Mary Celeste* was perfectly watertight and there was nothing to account for the disappearance of the crew. The ship's boats were still intact and the cargo (tallow and American clocks), was untouched. In due course, another part of the legend was added – that the breakfasts were all on the table about to be eaten. Since the weather was perfectly calm, the obvious mystery was what had caused the crew to abandon ship at a moment's notice on a calm morning. (This detail was taken from the captain's log.)

The true story of the *Mary Celeste* was as follows:

On a calm afternoon, December 5, 1872, the English ship *Dei Gratia* sighted a two-masted brig pursuing an erratic course in the north Atlantic, midway between the Azores and the coast of Portugal. As they came closer they could see that she was sailing with only her jib and foretop mast staysail set; moreover the jib was set to port, while the vessel was on a starboard tack – a sure sign to any sailor that the ship was out of control. Captain Moorehouse of the *Dei Gratia* signalled the mysterious vessel, but received no answer. The sea was running high after recent squalls, and it took a full two hours before Moorehouse could get close enough to read the name of the vessel. It was the *Mary Celeste*.

Moorehouse knew this American ship and its master, Captain Benjamin Spooner Briggs. Less than a month ago, both vessels had been loading cargo on neighboring piers on New York's East River. The *Mary Celeste* had set sail for Genoa with a cargo of crude alcohol on November 5, 1872, ten days before the *Dei Gratia* had sailed for Gibraltar; yet now, a month later, she was drifting in mid-Atlantic with no sign of life.

It took some time for the *Dei Gratia* to get close enough to the *Mary Celeste* to launch a boat – the sea was exceptionally rough. But at mid-afternoon, three seamen rowed across to the ship and two went aboard. They found that the *Mary Celeste* was deserted. Parts of the rigging had been blown away, and it was obvious that the ship had encountered a storm. The wheel was spinning free and the binnacle – the box containing the compass – had been knocked over and broken. The main hatch to below decks was secure, but some of the other hatch covers seemed to have been removed. There was roughly a foot of water in the galley, and plenty of food and supplies of fresh water. The lifeboat – not "boats" as Conan Doyle had stated – was missing, as were the chronometer, sextant and the navigation book. Clearly, Captain Briggs had decided to abandon ship at very short notice, and he expected to have to navigate his way back to land – in other words, he thought the *Mary Celeste* was sinking. It is not clear why he had not taken the ship's compass – this was found on board and was smashed. Below decks, sailors found that one of the casks of crude alcohol had been stoved in. The last entry in the log was dated November 25, ten days before the ship had been sighted by the *Dei Gratia*.

It was Captain Moorehouse's mate, Oliver Deveau, who persuaded him that they should sail the *Mary Celeste* back to Gilbraltar, and claim the £5,000 (or so) salvage money. Both ships arrived in Gibraltar harbor six days later. And instead of the welcome he expected, Deveau was greeted by an English bureaucrat who nailed an order of immediate arrest to the *Mary Celeste*'s mainmast. The date significantly was Friday 13th.

From the beginning, the *Mary Celeste* had been an unlucky ship. She was registered originally as the *Amazon*, and her first captain had died within 48 hours. On her maiden voyage she had hit a fishing weir off the coast of Maine and damaged her hull. While this was being repaired, a fire had broken out amidships. Later, while sailing through the Straits of Dover, she hit another brig which sank. This occurred under her third captain – her fourth accidentally ran the ship aground on Cape Brenton Island and wrecked her. The *Amazon* was salvaged, and passed through the hands of three more owners before she was bought by J.

H. Winchester, the founder of a successful shipping line which still operates in New York. Winchester discovered that the brig – which had by now been renamed *Mary Celeste* – had dry rot in her timbers, and he had the bottom rebuilt with copper lining and the deck cabin lengthened. These repairs had ensured that the ship was in excellent condition before she had sailed for Genoa under the experienced Captain Briggs – this helped to explain why she had survived so long in the wintery Atlantic, after the crew had taken to the lifeboat.

British officials at Gibraltar seemed to suspect either mutiny or some Yankee plot – the latter theory based on the fact that Captain Moorehouse and Captain Briggs had been friends, and had apparently dined together the day before the *Mary Celeste* had sailed from New York. But at the inquiry that followed, the idea of mutiny seemed to have gained favor. To back this theory, the Court of Inquiry was shown an axe-mark on one of the ship's rails, scoring on her hull that was described as a crude attempt to make the ship look as if she'd hit rocks, and a stained sword that was found beneath the captain's bunk. All this, it was claimed, pointed to the crew getting drunk, killing the master and his family and escaping in the ship's boat.

The Americans were insulted by what they felt was a slur on the honor of the US Merchant Navy, and indignantly denied the story. They pointed out that Briggs was not only known to be a fair man who was not likely to provoke the crew to mutiny, but also that he ran a dry ship – he was a New England puritan and the only alcohol on the *Mary Celeste* was its cargo. And even a thirsty sailor would not be likely to drink more than a mouthful of crude alcohol – being virtually methylated spirit, it would cause severe stomach pains and eventual blindness. Besides, if the crew had mutinied, why should they leave behind their seachests together with such items as family photographs, razors and sea-boots? The British admiralty remained unconvinced, but had to admit that if the alternative theory was correct and Briggs and Moorehouse had decided to make a false claim for salvage, Briggs would actually have lost by the deal – he was part-owner of the ship, and his share of any salvage would have come to a fraction of what he could have made by selling his share in the normal way.

In March 1873, the court was finally forced to admit that it was unable to decide why the *Mary Celeste* had been abandoned, the first time in its history that it had failed to come to a definite conclusion. The *Dei Gratia*'s owners were awarded one fifth of the value of the *Mary Celeste* and her cargo. The brig herself was returned to her owner, who lost no time in selling her the moment the ship got back to New York.

During the next eleven years, the *Mary Celeste* had many owners but brought little profit to any of them. Sailors were convinced she was unlucky and on the whole they were correct. Her last owner, Captain Gilman C. Parker, ran her aground on a reef in the West Indies and made a claim for insurance. The insurers became suspicious and Parker and his associates were brought to trial. At this time the penalty for deliberately scuttling a ship on the high seas was death by hanging, but the judge (mindful of the *Mary Celeste*'s previous record of bad luck), allowed the men to be released on a technicality. Within eight months Captain Parker was

The Mary Celeste

dead, one of his associates had gone mad and another had committed suicide. The *Mary Celeste* herself had been left to break up on the reef.

The brother of the *Mary Celeste*'s skipper, Captain James Briggs, was convinced that the clue lay in the last entry in the log. For the morning of November 25, 1872, it stated that the wind had dropped after a night of heavy squalls. James Briggs believed that the ship may have become becalmed in the Azores, and started to drift towards dangerous rocks on Santa Maria Island. The gash-marks found along the side of the *Mary Celeste* – which the British investigators had claimed were deliberately made by the ship's mutinous crew – may have been made when she actually rubbed against a submerged rock, convincing the crew that she was about to sink. Oliver Deveau proposed that during the storms some water had found its way up from between the decks into the hold, giving the impression that the ship was leaking.

Another popular explanation is that a waterspout hit the *Mary Celeste*. The atmospheric pressure inside a waterspout is low; this could have caused the hatch-covers to blow open, and force bilge water into the pump well. This would have made it look as if the ship had taken on six to eight feet of water and was sinking fast.

There are basic objections to all these three answers – if the ship scraped dangerous rocks off Santa Maria Island, then the lifeboat would have been close enough to land on the island. Since no survivors were found and no wreckage from the lifeboat either, this seems unlikely. Oliver Deveau's theory is more credible. There have often been panics at sea. When Captain Cook's *Endeavour* was in difficulties off the coast of eastern

Australia, the ship's carpenter was sent to take readings of the water in the hold. He made a mistake, and the resulting hysteria might have ended with the crew leaving the ship if Cook had not been able to control the panic. On another occasion, a ship which was carrying a hold full of timber dumped the whole lot into the sea off Newfoundland, before anyone realised that it would be next to impossible to sink a ship full of wood. But it seems unlikely that a captain of Briggs's known efficiency would allow such a simple misreading to cause a panic. The objection to the waterspout theory is that, apart from the open hatches, the ship was completely undamaged. If a waterspout was big enough to cause such a panic, it would surely have caused more havoc. In any case, the real mystery is why, if the crew left the *Mary Celeste* in the lifeboat, they made no attempt to get back on board when they saw that the ship was in no danger of sinking.

Only one explanation covers all the facts. Briggs had never shipped crude alcohol before, and being a typical New England puritan, knew very little about alcohol. The change in temperature between New York and the Azores would have caused casks of alcohol to sweat and leak. The night of storms, in which the barrels would have been shaken violently, would have caused vapor to form inside the casks, slowly building up pressure until the lids of some of them were blown off. The explosion, though basically harmless, might have blown the hatches off the cargo hold onto the deck in the positions in which Deveau later found them. Convinced that the whole ship was about to explode, Briggs ordered everyone into the lifeboat. In his haste, he failed to take the one simple precaution that would have saved their lives – to secure the lifeboat to the *Mary Celeste* by a few hundred yards of cable. Or perhaps he did so and the knot came undone. Or it is even possible that, in rowing away from the *Mary Celeste*, the other end of the cable was dropped by the sailor who was supposed to be securing it. The sea was fairly calm when the boat was lowered, as we know from the last entry in the log, but the evidence of the torn sails indicates that the ship then encountered severe gales. We may conjecture that the rising wind blew the *Mary Celeste* into the distance, while the crew in the lifeboat rowed frantically in a futile effort to catch up. And the lifeboat either sank in the heavy seas, or continued to drift until everybody aboard was dead.

In fact, the case of the Dutch schooner *Hermania* has a better title than the *Mary Celeste* to be regarded as one of the greatest mysteries of the sea. According to Commander Rupert Gould, in his book *The Stargazer Talks*, the *Hermania* was found drifting and deserted in 1849 – 23 years before the *Mary Celeste* – near the Eddystone Light off the coast of Cornwall. She was dismasted but still quite sound. The crew's possessions were found on board, and clothing that indicated that the captain's wife and child had also been on the ship. But the lifeboat was still lying in its chocks, undamaged. The only possible explanation seems to be that the whole crew was suddenly swept overboard by an enormous wave.

Deserted

Another mystery described in *The Stargazer Talks* is that of an unknown drifter encountered by the sailing vessel

Ellen Austin in the summer of 1881. Headed for St Johns, Newfoundland, the ship sighted a schooner in mid-Atlantic that seemed to be keeping a parallel course. As they came closer, they realised that the ship was drifting. A boarding party examined the schooner and everything seemed to be in order; there was no sign of struggle, but the crew was missing. The mate and several crew members from the *Ellen Austin* stayed on board to man the valuable prize, and for some time the two ships continued to sail parallel. Then a storm blew up driving them apart. When the storm had cleared, the mystery ship seemed to be damaged. The captain saw through his telescope that there was no one on deck. He ordered a boat to be lowered and went on board. The ship was once again deserted. His crew went into a panic. It took the captain a great deal of talking – and offers of reward – to persuade a four-man crew to go aboard the derelict. Again the two ships proceeded towards Newfoundland. The mystery schooner was faster than the *Ellen Austin* and soon drew ahead. That didn't bother the captain, however, because he expected to find the ship in St Johns when he arrived. There was no sign of the schooner in port. It had vanished along with the crew members.

In the *The Bermuda Triangle – Solved*, Lawrence David Kusche discusses the mystery and agrees that Commander Rupert Gould is a highly reliable researcher "who made authentic attempts to solve the mysteries that he encountered." But in spite of a lengthy search through the *New York Times Index* and the *Index* to the *Times* of London, Kusche was unable to find any information about the *Ellen Austin*. Neither was there any account in *The Newfoundlander* for 1881, although that paper "made a practice of describing interesting adventures of ships that docked in St Johns." Gould seems unlikely to have invented the story, but until someone can find the original account, it must be regarded as unverified.

According to Vincent Gaddis in *Invisible Horizons*, the mystery of the schooner *Zebrina* is equally baffling. In October 1917, the *Zebrina* left Falmouth, Cornwall, for France – a fairly short voyage. Two days later she was found drifting and deserted with no sign of violence or anything else to indicate why the crew had left. Gaddis says, "Everything aboard was shipshape, and her sails were set. The weather had been good for the relatively short voyage. Her crew had evidently been in the midst of a meal when something happened that caused the desertion, but there was not a clue on board as to this cause."

The only thing that seems clear is that, in mysteries like these, there is a fairly straightforward and down-to-earth explanation – nothing like the exotic story dreamed up by Conan Doyle to explain the desertion of the *Mary Celeste*.

Nevertheless, it must be admitted that some cases are so strange that they almost seem to invite a supernatural explanation. The strange case of the disappearing men of Eilean More is as baffling as the *Mary Celeste*, and, unlike that case, seems to defy all attempts at a logical explanation.

Washed out to Sea?

In the empty Atlantic, 17 miles to the west of the Hebrides, (west of Scotland), lie the Flannan Islands, known to seafarers as the Seven Hunters. The largest and most northerly of these is called Eilean Mor – which means in fact "big island." Like the *Mary Celeste*, its name has become synonymous with an apparently insoluble mystery of the sea.

These bleak islands received their name from a seventh-century bishop, St Flannan, who built a small chapel on Eilean Mor. Hebridean shepherds often ferried their sheep over to the islands to graze on the rich turf, but they themselves would never spend a night there for the islands are supposed to be haunted by spirits and by "little folk." In the last decades of the nineteenth century, as Britain's sea trade increased, many ships sailing north or south from Clydebank were wrecked on the Flannans, and in 1895 the Northern Lighthouse Board announced that a lighthouse would be built on Eilean Mor. They expected construction to take two years, but rough seas, and the problems of hoisting stones and girders up a 200-foot cliff, made it impossible to stick to the schedule; Eilean Mor lighthouse was finally founded on the rough seas between Lewis and the Flannans. Then, 11 days before Christmas 1900, the light went out.

The weather was too stormy for the Northern Lighthouse Board steamer to go and investigate, even though the lighthouse had been built with two landing-stages – one to the west and one to the east – so one of them would always be sheltered from the prevailing wind. Joseph Moore, waiting on the seafront at Loch Roag, had a sense of helplessness as he stared westward towards the Flannans. It was inconceivable that all three men on Eilean Mor – James Ducat, Donald McArthur and Thomas Marshall – could have fallen ill simultaneously, and virtually impossible that the lighthouse itself could have been destroyed by the storms.

On Boxing Day, 1900, the dawn was clear and the sea less rough. The *Hesperus* left harbor soon after daylight – Moore was so anxious that he refused to eat breakfast, pacing the deck and staring out towards the islands. The mystery had tormented him, and now he was too excited to take food. The swell was still heavy, and the *Hesperus* had to make three approaches before she was able to moor by the eastern jetty. No flags had answered their signals and there was no sign of life.

Moore was the first to reach the entrance gate. It was closed. He cupped his hands and shouted, then hurried up the steep path. The main door was closed and no one answered his shouts. Like the *Mary Celeste*, the lighthouse was empty. In the main room the clock had stopped and the ashes in the fireplace were cold. In the sleeping quarters upstairs – Moore waited until he was joined by two seamen before he ventured upstairs, afraid of what he might find there – the beds were neatly made, and the place was tidy. James Ducat, the chief keeper, had kept records on a slate. The last entry was for December 15 at 9.00 a.m., the day the light went out. But this had not been for lack of oil – the wicks were trimmed and the lights all ready to be lit. Everything was in order. So it was clear that the men had completed their basic duties for the day before tragedy struck them. When evening came there had been no one on the island to light the lamp. But the 15th of December had been a calm day . . . .

The *Hesperus* returned to Lewis with the men's Christmas presents still on board. Two days later, investigators landed on Eilean Mor and tried to reconstruct what had happened. At first it looked as if the solution was quite straightforward. On the westward jetty there was evidence of gale damage – a number of ropes were entangled round a crane which was 65-feet above sea-level. A tool chest kept in a crevice 45 feet above this was missing. It looked as if a hundred-foot wave had crashed in from the Atlantic and swept it away, as well as the three men. The fact that the oilskins belonging to Ducat and Marshall were missing seemed to support this theory (they only wore them to visit the jetties). So the investigators had a plausible theory. The two men had feared that the crane was damaged in the storm, they had struggled to the jetty in their oilskins, then been caught by a sudden huge wave . . . . But in that case, what had happened to the third man (Donald McArthur), whose oilskins were still in the lighthouse? Had he perhaps rushed out to try to save them and been swept away himself?

All these theories came crashing down when someone pointed out that the 15th had been a calm day – the storms had not started until the following day. Perhaps Ducat had simply entered the wrong date by mistake? That theory also had to be abandoned when, back at Loch Roag, Captain Holman of the *Archer* told them he had passed close to the islands on the night of the 15th, and that the light was already out . . . . Then, what if the three men had been on the jetty on a calm morning – which would explain why McArthur was not wearing his oilskins – and one of them had slipped into the water? Perhaps the other two had jumped in after him and been drowned. But then there were ropes and lifebelts on the jetty – why should men leap into the water when they only had to throw in a lifebelt? Suppose the drowning man was unconscious and could not grab a lifebelt? In that case, only one of his companions would have jumped in after him, leaving

111

the other on the jetty with a rope . . . . Another theory was that one of the three men had gone insane and pushed the others to their deaths, then thrown himself into the sea. It is just possible, but there is not the slightest shred of evidence for it.

The broadcaster Valentine Dyall – the "Man in Black" – suggested the most plausible explanation in his book, *Unsolved Mysteries*. In 1947, a Scottish journalist named Iain Campbell visited the Eilean Mor on a calm day, and was standing near the west landing when the sea suddenly gave a heave and rose 70 feet over the jetty. Then, after about a minute, it subsided back to normal. It could have been some freak of the tides, or possibly an underwater earthquake. Campbell was convinced that anyone on the jetty at that time would have been sucked into the sea. The lighthouse keeper told him that this curious "upheaval" occurs periodically and that several men had almost been dragged into the sea.

But it is still hard to understand how *three* men could be involved in such an accident. Since McArthur was not wearing his oilskins, we can presume he was in the lighthouse when it happened – *if* it happened. Even if his companions were swept away, would he be stupid enough to rush down to the jetty and fling himself into the sea? Only one thing is clear – that on that calm December day at the turn of the century, some accident snatched three men off Eilean Mor and left not even a shred of a clue to the mystery.

On June 29, 1968, Jerrold Potter and his wife Carrie climbed on board a DC-3 plane flying from Kankakee, Illinois to Dallas, Texas, to attend a Lion's Club convention. Potter was a 54-year-old insurance executive whose home background was secure and happy. The plane was north of Rolla, Missouri, when Potter stood up to go to the lavatory. On the way there he stopped to chat to James Schive, president of the Ottawa, Illinois, Lion's Club.

A few minutes after Potter had vanished into the lavatory, the plane shuddered slightly as if going through an air pocket but there were no more bumps. But Schive, sitting towards the back of the plane, noticed that when the plane quivered there was a rush of air.

After ten minutes or so, Mrs Potter began to wonder where her husband was and asked a stewardess to check the lavatory. The lavatory was empty but the rear door of the plane proved to be slightly ajar. And a piece of safety chain, which held it closed, was on the ground. The pilot had also noticed a warning light that a door was open and sent his co-pilot to check. He met the stewardess who had just found the door ajar.

Jerrold Potter had undoubtedly vanished from the plane by way of the rear door. Yet the event was still a total mystery. To begin with, the exit door had a warning in large white letters on a red background, "Do not open in flight." The door was secured with a heavy handle that had to be turned a full circle to release two huge bolts. In fact, the door was too heavy for the stewardesses to open and members of the crew always had to help. Yet Potter was a happy family man who had no reason to commit suicide. Why did he do it? For it must undoubtedly have been Potter himself who opened the door.

The plane had been flying over the Ozark Mountains when Potter disappeared and the body was never found.

Unexplained

We return to land for another of the most famous disappearances of all time. This is the way Charles Fort described it in *Lo!*:

"He walked around the horses.

"Upon November 25, 1809, Benjamin Bathurst, returning from Vienna, where, at the court of the Emperor Francis, he had been representing the British Government, was in the small town of Perleberg, Germany. In the presence of his valet and his secretary, he was examining the horses which were to carry his coach over more of his journey back to England. Under observation, he walked around to the other side of the horses. He vanished."

Fort says that he will keep the story short because it is already told by the Revd Sabine Baring-Gould in his book, *Historic Oddities* (1898). In fact, Baring-Gould's account differs in some respect from Fort's.

Benjamin Bathurst, born in 1784, was a British diplomat. Early in 1809, he went to Vienna as Ambassador Extraordinary, with the mission of persuading Austria to declare war on Napoleon. He succeeded, and the result was a disaster for Austria – Napoleon took Vienna in May, then defeated the Austrians in the Battle of Wagram in July. The Emperor Francis I was forced to sign a humiliating treaty at Znaim. Under the circumstances, there was nothing more for Bathurst to do and he set out for home. He decided to go via Berlin and North Germany. He carried pistols, for he was convinced that Napoleon would do his best to have him killed.

On November 25, 1809 (about midday), he arrived at Perleberg, *en route* from Berlin to Hamburg, and halted at the post house to order fresh horses for his coach, then walked a few yards to the White Swan Inn, kept by a man named Leger. It was beside the Parchimer gate of the town, through which Bathurst would later have to pass on his way to Lenzen, the next stop on the road. Bathurst ordered an early dinner, then inquired who was in charge of the soldiers. He was told that it was a Captain Klitzing, on the other side of the square. Bathurst called on Klitzing, said he thought he was in danger, and asked for a guard. A lady who was present noticed that he seemed to be in a state of considerable agitation, unable to raise a cup of tea to his lips without spilling some of it. The captain agreed, and let him have a couple of soldiers. At 7.00 p.m., Bathurst dismissed the guard and ordered the horses to be ready for 9.00 p.m. He stood at the door of the inn watching his portmanteau being replaced in the carriage, then stepped round the heads of the horses – and disappeared.

This was not quite as mysterious as Fort makes it sound. He did *not* walk around the horses in full view of other people – no one noticed him go. Moreover, it was a pitch black November evening. It was some time before anyone noticed that Bathurst was no longer at the inn. His secretary went to ask Captain Klitzing if he had seen him, but the answer was no. But Klitzing sent soldiers to seize the carriage, after which he transferred Bathurst's companions to an inn at the other end of town, with a guard over them. Klitzing had discovered that Bathurst's expensive fur coat was missing, and ordered a search for it. They found neither the coat nor its owner and it was not until three weeks later, on December 16, that two women gathering fuel in a small wood found a pair of gray trousers turned inside out. These were stained on the outside, as if the man who had worn them had been lying down on the grass. There were two bullet holes in the trousers but no trace of blood. The trousers were soon identified as those of Bathurst. A half-finished letter found in the pocket was addressed to Bathurst's wife, and said that he was afraid he would never reach England, and that if so, a man called the Count d'Entraigues was responsible. A large reward was offered by the British Government, and another by Bathurst's family. But no clue to Bathurst's whereabouts ever came to light.

On January 23, 1810, a Hamburg newspaper published a paragraph declaring that Bathurst had committed suicide in a fit of insanity. It also declared that his friends had received a letter from him, dated December 13, almost three weeks after his disappearance. All this proved to be untrue.

Meanwhile, the fur coat had finally been found in the cellar of a family named Schmidt, hidden behind firewood. Frau Schmidt said that it had been left at the post house, and that she had given it to her son Augustus – a man with a criminal record. Now Klitzing had found a witness who declared that she had seen Bathurst go down the narrow alleyway in which the Schmidts lived, so it was natural that suspicion fell upon them. Augustus Schmidt claimed that his mother had told him that the stranger had two pistols and had sent him to buy

The German town of Perleberg

some powder for them. He assumed that the stranger had shot himself.

No other evidence could be found against the Schmidts, and finally, Frau Schmidt and her son were sentenced to eight weeks in prison for the theft of the fur coat.

Bathurst's wife came to Perleberg in search of her husband, and interviewed a woman called Hacker, who was in jail for fraud. She claimed that in a nearby town called Seeberg, she met a shoemaker's assistant named Goldburger who came from Perleberg, and who was carrying a silk purse stuffed with gold. When she asked how he came by so much money he said that he had been given $500 to keep quiet "when the Englishman was murdered."

No one believed Frau Hacker, because everyone felt that she had probably concocted the story in some attempt to persuade Mrs Bathurst to help her get out of jail. But in fact, Frau Hacker may have known something about the disappearance. Her husband kept a tavern not far from the Swan Inn. Augustus Schmidt spent a great deal of his time there. Soon after Bathurst's disappearance, Hacker left Perleberg for Altona, near Hamburg, where he apparently had a great deal of money. It was also claimed that he had sold a gold repeater watch to a jeweller in Hamburg. In Perleberg, it was widely believed that Bathurst had been robbed and murdered by Hacker and Schmidt.

There was another view held by the citizens of Perleberg. Opposite the post house lived a man who had a reputation as being a spy paid by the French. Bathurst might well have fallen into conversation, have been persuaded to enter his house, and been murdered there for the diplomatic papers he was carrying.

Mrs Bathurst appealed to Napoleon, to see whether he could throw any light on her husband's disappearance, but Napoleon told her (through a go-between), that on his honor he knew nothing about it. Then in April 1852, 43 years after Bathurst's disappearance, a skeleton was found in a house that was being pulled down on the Hamburg Road. His skull had been fractured, as if by a blow. At the time of Bathurst's disappearance, the house had belonged to a man called Mertens, who was a servant at the Swan Inn. A sister of Bathurst hurried to Perleberg with a portrait of her brother, but was unable to say whether it was her brother's skull. All that was known about Mertens was that he was a hard-working man who had given his two daughters dowries of £150 and £120 – extremely large sums for a servant on low wages. Baring-Gould thinks that Mertens had something to do with Bathurst's disappearance. Certainly, his house was only about fifty yards away from the Swan Inn. He might easily have persuaded Bathurst to go a few steps with him, pretending he had something important to say, and then have lured Bathurst into his house where his skull was smashed with a blow from a hammer.

The most obvious solution is that Napoleon ordered the murder of Bathurst, not out of revenge, but out of a desire to lay hands on his diplomatic papers. But Baring-Gould points out that if Napoleon had ordered Bathurst to be robbed of his papers, he would almost certainly have given instructions to make it look as if it were a robbery by highwaymen, and allowed Bathurst to go.

Captain Klitzing remained firmly convinced that Bathurst had been killed during the course of a robbery – such a man must always have carried a fairly large sum of money on him.

In 1815, Earl Bathurst – who had sent Bathurst to Vienna – was Secretary of State for War and was one of those responsible for sending Napoleon to St Helena.

The likeliest explanation of the disappearance of Benjamin Bathurst is that Mertens played some part in it, but that he had probably been bribed by someone else – perhaps the French spy who lived opposite the inn. The French spy may also have bribed Augustus Schmidt. In some way, Mertens persuaded Bathurst to walk a few yards from the coach down a dark alley. There he was knocked over the head and taken to Mertens's house. Was he carrying the diplomatic papers that Napoleon was so anxious to get his hands on? Probably – he would regard them as the most valuable thing in his possession and never let them out of his sight. He would also be carrying a large sum of money in his diplomat's case. And so Mertens – and possibly Schmidt – got the money, Schmidt got the fur coat, and the French spy got the papers.

It is a pity that the solution should be so prosaic. The notion of a man walking around the horses and then vanishing into thin air is much more romantic. Charles Fort obviously prefers this view, "In the presence of his valet and his secretary, he was examining horses . . . . under observation, he walked around to the other side of the horses. He vanished." But Fort, who had read Baring-Gould's account, knew perfectly well that Bathurst was *not* under observation when he walked around the horses. (In fact, according to the memoirs of his father, Bishop Bathurst, published in 1837, it was a full hour before Bathurst's disappearance was noticed.) Fort obviously subscribed to the view of the newspaper editor who said, "Never let the facts spoil a good story."

Victor Grayson was only 25 when he became a Member of Parliament for Colne Valley, a grim millworking area, and was good-looking as well as a brilliant orator – his female constituents swooned over him. He spent most of his time travelling around the country urging workers to go on strike, and made no secret of his opinion that most of his fellow MPs were dishonest time-servers.

Within four years he was fast becoming an alcoholic, and was sometimes drunk on the platform. By 1914 his career seemed to be over. By that time he was married to an actress, and in 1916 they sailed for Australia, where he joined the army, later serving with bravery in France.

Back in England in 1918, he became a widower and began to live a strange existence as an associate of the swindler Horatio Bottomely and the amiable homosexual con-man Maundy Gregory, who helped the Prime Minister Lloyd George raise cash for his party by selling honours – £40,000 for a peerage and £10,000 for a knighthood. No one knows quite what Grayson did for a living, but he seemed reasonably well-off.

Then he vanished. On a pleasant summer evening in 1920 two men called to see him at his servico flat in a Georgian House, central London – the housekeeper thought they were 'not gentlemen.' Grayson told her he would be back soon – and vanished.

An artist painting a Thames scene near Ditton Island claimed he saw Grayson the next day – he recognised him – going into a bungalow on the island. It turned out to be Maundy Gregory's bungalow, and some writers on the mystery speculate that Gregory lured him there and killed him, dumping his heavily-weighted body in the river.

Yet there were many 'sightings' over the years; one man saw him from the top of a bus, another claimed Grayson had taken him for a drink after a political meeting.

One theory is that Grayson was involved in the honours scandal – for which Gregory went to prison for two months in 1933 – and was paid to disappear by the British government.

But it may have been simpler than that. Grayson had what was, for those times, a scandalous secret. Letters discovered in 1983 revealed that in his early days, had had a homosexual affair with a young 'comrade', Harry Dawson.

If Grayson was, in fact, primarily homosexual, then his alcoholism may be explained by the psychological tension of feeling that he was being forced to live a lie.

The MP Ernest Marklew claimed that in 1939, he had traced Grayson to a furniture shop in London, which Grayson owned, and that Grayson told him he wanted to vanish into anonymity.

The reason, many now believe, is that Grayson wanted to live quietly with a male lover, and that he simply changed his name and 'dropped out.'

5

A Lapse of Memory

Most people are unaware of how many people per year disappear as a result of sudden loss of memory – according to the writer Jay Robert Nash, in his book Among the Missing, *no less than 20,000 Americans per year suffer from amnesia.*

No one really understands this illness. There was a time when it was believed that one particular compartment of the brain contains our memory, and so it is easy to suppose that if some minor problem – like a burst blood vessel – affects that part, the "memory tapes" of our own past might be completely wiped, or at least made inaccessible. But we now know that there is no specific part of the brain that deals with memory. All attempts to pin down such a part – by removing different parts of the brain of an animal in an attempt to cause it to forget something it has learned – have so far failed. It looks as if memory is somehow spread throughout the whole brain.

One of the earliest – and oddest – cases of memory-loss was described by the nineteenth-century psychologist, William James.

The Reverend Ansel Bourne was a preacher who lived in Greene, Rhode Island. On the morning of January

17, 1887, Bourne went into Providence and drew out from his bank the odd sum of $551, paid some bills and took a horse-car from Pawtucket, 20 miles away. Then he vanished. His worried family searched for him in Providence and placed advertisements in local newspapers. There seemed no obvious reason why Bourne should have disappeared – he was a perfectly happy family man, devoted to his Christian mission. The family suspected he might have been murdered for the money he was carrying. In fact, 200 miles away in Norristown, Pennsylvania, two weeks later, a man who called himself A. J. Brown rented a store that sold stationery, confectionery and fruit. He attended church every Sunday, and one day was asked to make a speech in church, which he did with commendable fluency. His fellow church goers were surprised, for Brown seemed to be an exceptionally timid man.

On March 14, two months after disappearing, Brown woke up in a strange state of confusion. He walked out of his store in Norristown saying he could not understand what he was doing there – his real name was Ansel Bourne and he lived in Greene, Rhode Island. His neighbors naturally thought that he had gone mad, but they nevertheless telegraphed Greene to humor him. They were amazed to discover that Brown had been telling the truth – he really was the Reverend Ansel Bourne. Bourne had no memory whatsoever of how he came to be in Norristown and why he had rented a store. He could not even remember drawing the $551 out of the bank. He simply went back to Greene – now something of a celebrity – and resumed work as a preacher.

Three years later, in 1890, William James went to call

on him. He wanted to persuade Bourne to be hypnotized and try to find out what hidden personality had taken him over for two months. Under hypnosis, James was able to make contact with Mr A. J. Brown and to talk to him about the two months in Norristown. Brown told James that he had heard of Bourne but added that "he had never met the man." James had to conclude that there were two people living inside Bourne's body, like R. L. Stevenson's Dr Jekyll and Mr Hyde. The case led James to propound his theory of the "stream of consciousness." He said that consciousness has continuity in exactly the same sense as a river. When we wake up in the morning, we remember the person who went to sleep last night – because he is only slightly further back up the river. But if something interrupts the flow of the river, diverting it elsewhere, then this normal sense of continuity is interrupted. It is an interesting theory, but it seems to contradict something we all feel quite basically – that we contain a single "self." It is true that I can go into a room to get something, and then forget what I have gone in for, but this is only a minor interruption of the stream of consciousness. To lose a whole section of the personality is obviously far more serious.

The French psychologist, Pierre Janet, made an interesting discovery in the 1880s when studying a patient he called Irene. Irene used to sleepwalk and had periods of amnesia. Janet discovered that it had all started when her mother, to whom she was deeply attached, was dying from consumption. For two months, Irene struggled to cope, working by day and nursing her mother by night. When her mother died she was shattered. She even tried to make the corpse breathe again. Then her mother fell out of bed and Irene had a difficult task lifting her back in. It was after this that Irene began to have periods of amnesia. Under hypnosis, Janet was able to access another part of her personality and realised what had happened – Irene found the whole memory of her mother's illness and death so painful that she managed to block it out completely. What Janet had discovered – some years before Freud made the same discovery – was that under stress, certain parts of the personality can (so to speak) "blow a fuse" and apparently disappear.

James was greatly intrigued by another case of amnesia – a man called the Reverend Thomas Hanna, who lost his memory after being knocked unconscious when he fell down climbing out of a carriage. When he woke up, he had, in effect, reverted to childhood. He did not even remember how to eat, and had to be gradually trained to chew food that was put into his mouth. He had to learn to talk all over again. His memory came back one night after a profound sleep, but he told his psychiatrists that in this sleep, he suddenly confronted his two different personalities and had to decide which of them he wished to keep. The real problem, he said, was that he did not feel that he could choose one and ignore the other. He said he was not sufficiently ruthless to kill off one part of himself. But eventually, he had to make the painful choice and became more or less his former self.

But many cases of amnesia seem to have no obvious cause. Luther Maynard Jones was a brilliant and successful lawyer in New York in the last decades of the nineteenth century. He was also one of its most famous art collectors, and became such an expert that the

Metropolitan Museum of Art tried to persuade him to join the staff. In 1897, when Jones was 60, his partner suggested that he ought to take a trip to Europe to refresh his mind. Jones took his advice – and disappeared. Twelve years later, a former classmate suddenly recognised Jones on a London street. But when he spoke to him, Jones denied his identity and said that his name was simply Luther Maynard. He had never heard of anyone called Jones. And he firmly declined all invitations to go back to New York and take up his old life. Three years later, when Jones was 73, he was tracked down to the Streatham Hill Workhouse in London. He still had no memory whatsoever of his life as a lawyer in New York. Friends who determined to bring him back to America and collected money for that purpose, were frustrated when Jones died suddenly. His last words were, "Who am I then, please? Who?"

Jay Robert Nash cites the even stranger case of Dr William Horatio Bates, a famous eye specialist in New York who vanished in 1902. He disappeared on August 30, but wrote to his wife assuring her that he had simply gone out of town to do some major operations that would bring him a great deal of money. After that, she heard from him no more. Six weeks later, she received an anonymous letter telling her that her husband was now studying medicine in a London hospital. She hastened to England and found him in the Charing Cross Hospital. But he did not recognise her and recalled nothing of their marriage. Thoroughly upset, Mrs Bates returned to New York and died three years later – holding a portrait of her husband. Then, in

1911 – nine years after his disappearance – Dr Bates came back to New York, his memory apparently now restored, and resumed his practice as an eye specialist. He was able to say that he had wandered through Europe suffering from amnesia but that he could remember nothing else. One of his friends remarked, "It was as if he had had a chunk of his mind removed, like a slice of watermelon chopped away and eaten by an invisible monster." But at least Dr Bates once again became a successful eye surgeon and maintained his identity until he died.

On the evening of May 15, 1970, Mr and Mrs Edward Andrews of Arlington Heights, near Chicago, attended a cocktail party in the Chicago Sheraton Hotel – they had been given tickets by a friend. During the evening, 63-year-old Andrews was heard to complain of being hungry having eaten only cocktail canapes. He seems to have taken out his irritation on his wife, who was seen to be crying before the end of the party. When it was over, at about 9.30 p.m., they went down to the underground garage of the hotel and drove off in their 1969 Oldsmobile. They drove away on lower Michigan Avenue, towards the bridge across the Chicago river. That was the last time they were ever seen. Since the couple were childless, there were no heirs to their expensive house and more than adequate bank account.

The police theorized that Andrews may have had a blackout at the wheel and plunged the car into the Chicago river. But the river was thoroughly dragged and no sign of the car was found. Their disappearance remains a mystery.

Nash also recounts the delightful case of Benjamin Levy, a Brooklyn baker who disappeared in 1924. Two years later, a friend walked into an office block, and found Levy sweeping the floor.

"Hello, Ben, where have you been for two years?"

Levy stopped sweeping and said with astonishment, "You mean me?"

His friend said, "You're Ben Levy. You've been missing for more than two years."

"You're nuts, Buddy. Beat it."

The friend called the police and Levy was taken to the police station. His wife, daughter and family doctor arrived and all recognized him.

"You're all crazy," said Levy. "My name is Frank Lloyd. I'm not a Jew, I'm a Roman Catholic. And I've never been married."

"You own a bakery in Brooklyn," Levy's daughter Esther said.

Levy shook his head. "I work as a day laborer. I wouldn't know a baker's oven if I saw one."

Mrs Levy produced a letter she had received during the past two years. "You say here in your own handwriting that you are a prisoner on a rum-running ship in New York harbour. Don't you remember writing this?"

"Of course I don't."

A policeman recalled how half the force had been searching ships in New York harbor looking for Levy at the time he wrote the letter. To try to prove to him that he was really Levy, the police insisted on taking his fingerprints and comparing them with the known fingerprints of the baker. They matched exactly.

"Come on back home Ben," said his wife.

"I ain't Ben!" shouted Levy. "I work as a porter. I've been sweeping out saloons and offices for years. Ask anybody."

Mrs Levy also lost her temper. "You are Benjamin Levy and you're my husband. Come home this instant!"

"Lady, I don't doubt you think I'm Mr Levy. But I'm not."

"Don't call me 'lady.' I'm Helen, your wife."

"Maybe you are my wife, but I don't remember a thing about it."

It was then that Levy's 17-year-old nephew walked into the room and said, "Oh hi, Uncle Benny!" Levy began to look half convinced. "Well," he said, "maybe you're right, but I certainly don't remember anything about it." Ben Levy allowed himself to be persuaded to go home with his wife and daughter, and once again took up his life as a baker. No one ever discovered why he had lost his memory.

One famous case of amnesia had considerable political impact. Raymond Robins had become rich by discovering gold in the Klondike at the turn of the century, and when he moved to the east coast of America he became well known for his charitable social work and his detestation of alcohol. He became one of the most prominent crusaders for Prohibition in America and was instrumental in the passing of the Volstead Act in 1919, which suddenly plunged America into teetotalism and gangsterism.

On the evening of September 3, 1932, Colonel Raymond Robins ate a meal at the City Club in West 44th Street, Manhattan, with another passionate Prohibitionist, Daniel Poling, and they almost certainly discussed the probability that Prohibition would be repealed after the next election. Robins left the club early – around 7.00 p.m. – and then vanished. He was due to go to the White House for a conference with President Herbert Hoover the following Tuesday, about a nationwide speaking tour in support of the President and Prohibition, and when he failed to appear, Hoover himself ordered a search for him. It was widely suspected that he had been murdered by gangsters – many of whom had threatened to kill him. Others thought that he might have disappeared to the Soviet Union, since he was known to be enthusiastic about that regime. There was a rumor that rumrunners had kidnapped him and thrown him into the sea off Montauk, Long Island. But although every newspaper reporter in the country was searching for him, no one was able to come up with a clue to his disappearance.

What did happen was that a man calling himself Reynolds Rogers, wearing overalls and a hunting cap, knocked on the door of a boarding-house run by a Mrs W. E. Bryson in Balsam, North Carolina (a small mountain village), and asked for lodgings. He told Mrs Bryson that he was a miner from Harlan, Kentucky, and that he intended to prospect for gold in the hills of North Carolina. Since Mrs Bryson was fairly certain that the hills of North Carolina did not contain any gold, she wrote him off as an eccentric. But Rogers paid his rent and the next morning went out searching for gold. When he returned that evening, he learned that a man from Miami, Florida, was staying in the boarding-house. He became obviously nervous and two

131

days later moved to another boarding-house. Before he took a room there, he enquired whether there was anybody from Miami staying there. During the next two months, Rogers became a familiar sight wandering around the hills of North Carolina, often stopping for a chat with farmers who then – as now – concocted moonshine whisky in their private stills. He often mentioned that he knew President Theodore Roosevelt and President Herbert Hoover, but admitted that he could not remember how he met them. He also became a trusted friend of the Cherokee Indians and delivered talks to their children. He had become an accepted part of the community when a thirteen-year-old boy named Fisher happened to see a newspaper photograph of the missing Colonel Robins, and realised that he was the same man as Reynolds Rogers. In no time at all, crowds of reporters and doctors had descended on the boarding-house in Whittier where he was staying.

Like Ben Levy, Rogers vigorously denied that he was Colonel Robins, or that he knew anything about him. "I just want to be left alone," he said pathetically. When Mrs Robins arrived, she burst into tears.

"You say this is my wife?" Rogers asked one of the doctors.

"Yes, this is Mrs Robins."

Robins – who was now wearing a heavy beard – stared at his wife and signs of conflict were visible upon his face. After several minutes of silence he suddenly turned to the psychiatrist and said, "Doctor I *am* Raymond Robins, and this is my wife Margaret Dreier Robins." Mrs Robins told the reporters that her husband looked at her and that his face changed very slowly. Then he called her Margaret, and it was obvious that he was suddenly his old self. Again, no one ever explained this famous disappearance – except for saying that it was a case of amnesia. But it was suggested that his obvious nervousness about the fellow lodger from Miami was due to the fact that Florida bootleggers had sworn to kill Colonel Robins.

The obviously puzzling part of all these stories is exactly what the amnesiac thought when he suddenly discovered that he no longer had any memory of his past. Why do such people not hurry to the nearest doctor and explain that they have lost their memory? It seems that some deep-seated defence mechanism prevents them from acknowledging that they have no past – either that, or they actually believe that they are somebody else. There are a few bold psychiatrists who have suggested that perhaps multiple personality is genuinely a case of several different people living in the same body, most of them suppressed by the "dominant personality." But this is not a question that can be discussed here in this book.

Perhaps the most horrific story of amnesia concerns a man called Harry Miller, of Salt Lake City, who lost twenty years of his life. When he woke up in a prison cell, the last thing he remembered was that he had left Salt Lake City, enlisted in the army, and was waiting to report to his camp. But on his way there, he was waylaid by thugs and knocked unconscious. He sat up in the cell, rubbed the bump on his head and called to a guard outside the door, "Did you get those guys who stole my wallet?" The guard told him that he was in prison because he had been riding a freight-car when a policeman had found him, and had started to fight. The policeman had hit him on the head with his truncheon, which is why he was in prison. The bewildered Miller saw that the guard was carrying a newspaper and asked if he could see it. When Miller saw the date, he went pale. "1937! But this is 1917! Is this a joke?" There was a battered mirror hanging in the corner of the cell, and Miller went and looked in it. He was horrified to see the face of an old bum with white hair and several days growth of beard on his chin. He had no memory whatever of what had happened to him since being knocked unconscious by the thugs who had taken his wallet. In the meantime, he had obviously become a tramp and wandered the country, until the blow on the head from the policeman brought back his memory. Unfortunately, Jay Robert Nash, who tells the story, seems to have no idea of what became of Miller.

In 1926, England had its own equivalent of the Colonel Robins case. It involved the novelist Agatha Christie. At the age of thirty-six, Agatha Christie was an attractive redhead who lived with her husband, Colonel Archibald Christie, in a magnificent country house, which she once described as "a sort of millionaire-style Savoy suite transferred to the country." She was already a moderately known detective writer and her latest novel, *The Murder of Roger Ackroyd*, had caused a certain amount of angry controversy because of its "unfair" ending – the murderer turns out to be the man who narrates the story.

On a freezing cold night, December 3, 1926, she walked out of her country home at Sunningdale (in Berkshire), and vanished. At 11 a.m. the next morning,

Agatha Christie

a Superintendent of the Surrey Police was handed a report on a "road accident" at Newlands Corner, just outside Guildford, where Agatha Christie's Morris 2-seater had been found halfway down a grassy bank with its bonnet buried in a clump of bushes. There was no sign of the driver, but she had clearly not intended to go far because she had left her fur coat in the car. By mid-afternoon, the press had heard of the disappearance and were clamoring at the front door of her country home. The police – perhaps aware of rumors that the Colonel was being unfaithful to his wife – hinted at suicide, but Colonel Christie dismissed the idea, pointing out that people usually commit suicide at home. Nevertheless, the Silent Pool, near the scene of the "accident", was searched by deep-sea divers.

In fact, Colonel Christie had recently fallen in love with a girl who was ten years his junior – Nancy Neele – and had recently told Agatha Christie that he wanted a divorce. The death of her mother had been another recent psychological shock. She was sleeping badly, eating erratic meals, and moving furniture around the house in a haphazard manner. She was obviously distraught, possibly on the verge of a nervous breakdown. The two or three days hereafter produced no clues to her whereabouts. When it was reported that some female clothes had been found in a lonely hut near Newlands Corner, together with a bottle labelled "opium", there was a stampede of journalists. But it proved to be a false alarm and the opium turned out to be a harmless stomach remedy. Some newspapers hinted that Archibald Christie stood much to gain from the death of his wife, but he had a perfect alibi – he was at a weekend party in Surrey. Other journalists began to wonder whether the disappearance was a publicity stunt. Lord Ritchie-Calder suspected that she had disappeared to spite her husband and bring his affair with Nancy Neele out into the open. He even read through her novels to see whether she had used a similar scenario. When the *Daily News* offered a reward, reports of sightings poured in. They all proved to be false alarms.

Another interesting touch of mystery was added when her brother-in-law, a man named Campbell, revealed that he had received a letter from her whose postmark indicated that it had been posted in London at 9.45 a.m. on the day after her disappearance, when she had been presumed to be wandering in the woods of Surrey. In the *Daily Mail* the following Sunday, there was an interview with her husband in which he admitted "that my wife had discussed the possibility of disappearing at will. Some time ago she told her sister, 'I could disappear if I wished and set out it carefully . . . .'"

On December 14, 1926, eleven days after her disappearance, the head waiter in the Hydropathic Hotel in Harrogate, North Yorkshire, looked more closely at a female guest and recognized her from newspaper photographs as the missing novelist. He rang the Yorkshire Police, who contacted her home. Colonel Christie took an afternoon train from London to Harrogate and learned that his wife had been staying in the hotel for a week and a half. She had taken a good room on the first floor at seven guineas a week, had apparently seemed "normal and happy", and "sang, danced, played billiards, read the newspaper reports of her disappearance, chatted with her fellow guests, and went for walks."

Agatha Christie was sitting at the dinner table, reading an evening newspaper which contained the story of the search for her – including a photograph – when her husband came and joined her. "She only seemed to regard him as an acquaintance whose identity she could not quite fix", said the hotel manager. And Archibald Christie told the Press. "She has suffered from the most complete loss of memory, and I do not think she knows who she is." A doctor later confirmed that she was suffering from loss of memory. But Lord Ritchie-Calder later remembered how little she seemed to correspond with the usual condition of amnesia. When she vanished, she had been wearing a green knitted skirt, a grey cardigan and a velour hat, and carried a few pounds in her purse. When she was found, she was stylishly dressed and had £300 on her. She told other guests in the hotel that she was a visitor from South Africa.

There were unpleasant repercussions. A public outcry, orchestrated by the Press, wanted to know who was to pay the £3,000 which the search was estimated to have cost and Surrey rate-payers blamed the next big increase in rates on her. Her novel *The Big Four* received unfriendly reviews but nevertheless sold 9,000 copies – more than twice as many as *The Murder of Roger Ackroyd*. And from then on (as Elizabeth Walter has described in an essay called "The case of the escalating sales"), her books sold in increasing quantities. By 1950, all her books were enjoying a regular sale of more than 50,000 copies and the final Miss Marple story, *Sleeping Murderer* had a first printing of 60,000 copies.

Agatha Christie divorced her husband (who wed Miss Neele), and in 1930 married Professor Sir Max Mallowan, the archaeologist. But for the rest of her life she refused to discuss her disappearance and would only grant interviews on condition that it was not mentioned. Her biographer, Janet Morgan, accepts that it was a case of nervous breakdown followed by amnesia. Yet this fails to explain how she obtained the clothes and the money to get to Harrogate. Moreover, she had registered in the hotel under the name of Nancy Neele, her husband's mistress.

Lord Ritchie-Calder, who got to know her very well in later life, remains convinced that "her disappearance was calculated in the classic style of her detective stories." In other words, that it was a publicity stunt. A television play produced after her death even speculated that her disappearance was part of a plot to murder Nancy Neele. It was certainly fortunate for her that the publicity surrounding her disappearance turned her into a bestselling author. Yet after looking at the other cases in this chapter, it is quite possible to believe that she suffered from the same kind of amnesia as Ansel Bourne or Colonel Robins and that as she read about the disappearance of Agatha Christie in newspapers, she remained absolutely convinced that it was all nothing to do with her. Such are the strange complexities of the human mind.

Another writer who suffered a bout of amnesia was Sherwood Anderson, who achieved sudden fame in 1919 with his book, *Winesburg, Ohio*. But it was seven years earlier when he suffered a loss of memory.

Anderson had been born in Camden, Ohio, in 1876. When he was twenty, he went to Chicago and worked as a laborer. After a brief period serving as a soldier in the Spanish-American War, he returned to Chicago and went into advertising, working as a copywriter. He moved to Elyria, Ohio, where he ran a paint manufacturing business until it collapsed.

In 1912, when he was 36, Anderson felt that his life had been a failure. He was married to a schoolteacher named Cornelia and had three children, but the five years struggle to keep the paint manufacturing business going had taken their toll. He was becoming exhausted and discouraged.

On the afternoon of November 27, 1912, he was dictating a letter to his secretary, and had just spoken the words, "The goods about which you have enquired are the best of their kind made in the . . . ." when suddenly he went silent. His secretary looked at him and saw that his face had become blank. When she asked what was the matter, Anderson replied, "My feet are cold and wet. I've been walking too long on the bed of a river." Then, he suddenly seemed to change personality, buttoned his coat and strode vigorously from the office.

For more than three days, the police searched for him, and then he was found in Cleveland, Ohio, in a drug-store. He was obviously in a state of bewilderment and had apparently been wandering around for four days, sleeping under hedges, no longer knowing who he was. He was taken by friends to the Huron Road Hospital but had no memory whatever of what had happened after dictating the sentence. To the end of his life, he was unable to remember.

He returned to Chicago, went back to his old job of advertising, and became a friend of various writers like Theodore Dreiser and Carl Sandburg. A novel published in 1916, *Windy McPherson's Son*, and *Marching Men*

(1917), failed to make any impact, but his book of short stories, *Winesburg, Ohio* (1919), immediately made him famous. This story of a small town and its suffocating respectability became a favorite of the younger generation, and his simple and straightforward style influenced writers like Ernest Hemingway and John Steinbeck.

Sadly, Anderson died at the age of 64, in 1941, from swallowing a cocktail stick stuck through an *hors d'oeuvre* sausage, which gave him peritonitis. Typically, the headline in the local newspaper in Elyria, where he had suffered his amnesia, read "Sherwood Anderson, former Elyria manufacturer, dies." Anderson's unsuccessful paint business, which had almost cost him his sanity, dogged him beyond the grave.

In the year 1763, Owen Parfitt, a citizen of Shepton Mallet, Somerset, vanished without trace. As a young man he had served as a soldier in America and lived a life of intrigue and adventure. Back in England, he had worked as a tailor until suffering a stroke. Emaciated to a skeleton and confined to bed, he was looked after by his neighbors and his elderly sister. "By his own desire," the Reverend Collinson wrote, "he had several times been brought down stairs in an elbow chair, and placed in the passage of the house for the benefit of the air. In this situation he was left one evening for a few minutes, but on his attendant's return this helpless man was missing, nowhere to be found — nor has he since been heard of." Within sight of the cottage, haymakers were busy but they testified that no one had passed them by and nothing unusual had happened.

Some have speculated that Shepton Mallet, about eight miles from Glastonbury, may occupy a vortex or area of magnetic or climatic disturbance which facilitates such abberrations. Collinson's attitude, however, was more hard-headed. He believed Parfitt had somehow struggled to his feet and wandered through by-paths, "till falling into some pool, pit or cavern, his appearance and existence upon earth were at once terminated together."

Fifty years later, a report appeared in the *Western Flying Post* concerning the digging up of a skeleton at Board Cross, "not far from that, whence a pauper, named Owen Parfitt, was very unaccountably removed about 50 years ago . . . . The proportion of the bones, and the position of the whole, warrant a conclusion that the remains of Owen Parfitt are at length discovered; and thus the weakness of superstition, and daring assertions of impiety, are deservedly set at naught."

The matter is hardly set at rest by such a summary dismissal. No evidence is produced to identify the skeleton with that of Parfitt's and the reporter writes as if the whole incident had not only annoyed him, but undermined the authority of religion.

Another writer who disappeared – although not, as far as we know, suffering from amnesia – was Ambrose Bierce. Bierce was also born in Ohio, in 1842, and was always ashamed of his sternly religious parents. He spent a year at a military academy and enlisted on the Union side in the Civil War. But he came to doubt the justice of the cause for which he was fighting and when offered a large sum in back pay after the war, refused it, saying, "When I hired out as an assassin for my country, that wasn't part of the contract."

After the war he moved to San Francisco, taking a job as a night-watchman at the Mint, then managing to become a columnist on a local newspaper. As a critic, his tongue could be deadly and he could make or break a book. In 1868 he became editor of *The Newsletter*, in which he published his first short story in 1871. Among his friends in San Francisco were Mark Twain and Bret Harte. With $10,000 (given to him by his father-in-law as a wedding present), Bierce and his wife went to England in 1872 and stayed there for four years. He was in Leamington during this period, so his curious tale of the cobbler, James Worson, who disappeared as he stumbled to the ground could well be something that he read in a local newspaper.

In 1876, after achieving literary success in London, he returned to San Francisco and soon regained his former celebrity as a journalist.

In 1886, a young man named William Randolph Hearst took over the San Francisco *Examiner* from his father and hired Bierce to write his "Prattler" column for that newspaper. Over the next ten years, Bierce published some of his best work in the paper, including some short stories. But his characteristic tone was bitter and savage, earning him the nickname "Bitter Bierce." In *The Devil's Dictionary*, he defines a cynic as "a blackguard whose faulty vision sees things as they are, not as they ought to be."

Bierce obviously felt that, in taking the lowest possible view of human brings, he was seeing them accurately. So his other definitions include "Bore: a person who talks when you wish him to listen,"

"Egotist: a person of low taste, more interested in himself than in me," "Admiration: our polite recognition of another man's resemblance to ourselves." A typical witticism is, "Calamities are of two kinds: misfortune to ourselves, and good fortune to others." Understandably, many people detested him. His wife divorced him for cruelty.

As Bierce approached the age of 70, he became increasingly cantankerous and restive. The thought of succumbing to decay enraged him. His life had been adventurous and tragic – one son had committed suicide and another died of drink – and there is evidence that he himself planned deliberately to die with his boots on. In 1913, he decided to revisit the battlefields of the Civil War (about which he had written brilliantly), and then go on to Mexico where there was also a civil war, and perhaps on to South America. In fact, Bierce so impressed the Mexican bandit-turned-revolutionary, Pancho Villa, that Villa issued the writer with credentials to accompany him as a war correspondent. Bierce's last letter was written from Chihuahua, Mexico, on December 26, 1913. Then silence. Ever since then, investigators have produced "authentic" accounts of what happened. One declared that Bierce had lost his temper with Villa and told him he was nothing but a cut-throat, whereupon Villa had instantly ordered his execution. Another said that he had been killed in the siege of Ojinago, and that his death had been reported in Mexican army dispatches. One of his friends in Washington always insisted that he had blown out his brains on a high ledge of the Grand Canyon and then fallen into its depths ("an appropriate tombstone for his gigantic ego.") But the

Ambrose Bierce

most bizarre story is that he was captured by a wild tribe in southern Mexico and boiled alive, after which his shrunken remains had been worshipped. This is clearly the version that Bierce himself would have chosen.

Perhaps the saddest of all amnesia cases on record concerns an American soldier from World War I who had been gassed and shot, as a consequence of which he suffered total amnesia. One day he found himself in the California Insane Asylum with no idea how he had got there. All he could remember was that he had once been on the Western Front in World War I. A judge had given him the name Jerry Tarbot – presumably after he had appeared in court for vagrancy. He began looking for his identity in various hospitals and military camps. A doctor called Samuel Marcus hypnotized him and succeeded in regressing him to World War I, but the result was that Tarbot thought he was digging trenches and tried to dig holes in the carpet. As a result of all the publicity about the hypnosis, many soldiers who remembered him came forward. But none of them could remember his name. One recorded seeing him at Verdun in a marine uniform and said that he was known as "the sliding ghost" because of his ability to slide through enemy territory. Dr Marcus decided that Tarbot was a New Yorker, and approached the Marine Corps General Neville, who vaguely remembered that the man had served with the Marine brigade at Belleau Wood. Tarbot worked his way to the East Coast on a tramp steamer, but arrived in Washington so ill that he had to be put in hospital for seven months. It was while he was there that, looking at a case of surgical instruments, he suddenly remembered that he had once worked at making surgical instruments in a Brooklyn shop. He hurried to New York and recognised the J. Sklar Manufacturing Company as the place where he had once worked. Again, many workers in the shop recognized him but none could remember his name. And the records dating back to pre-war days had been destroyed.

One day Tarbot recalled that he had served Mass in the chapel at Fordham University in his teens. Father Henry McGarvey recalled Tarbot but again could not remember his name. The case was now exciting such wide-spread interest that the New York Missing Person's Bureau assigned some of its employees to try and help Tarbot, but nothing came of it. The records of the French and Canadian Army also failed to produce results. On October 14, 1923, thousands of Legionnaires gathered for their annual convention in Philadelphia and Tarbot went up on stage to ask them whether anyone recognized him. After a long silence, a voice called, "Yes, I know you." A Legionnaire named Benjamin Sprang from Philadelphia, climbed up on stage, but yet again, although Sprang could remember all kinds of details about Tarbot, he could not remember his name. At least Sprang's memories suddenly brought back a brief flash of recollection – Tarbot remembered going into action with a platoon lead by Lieutenant Robinson. More memories of that day came back, including being blown up by a grenade. Two mothers whose sons had disappeared during the war came up to look at Tarbot, but both shook their heads and turned away. In the ensuing publicity, three more men came forward, one declaring that Jerry Tarbot was actually called James Talbot who had worked with him in Havana, Cuba. But that had been since the war. But another of the men who came forward identified Tarbot as a French-Canadian called George Beaupré. Yet another man said that Tarbot's real name was Bruce Harpin, who owned a lunch-counter in Brooklyn. Another flash of memory sent Tarbot to Akron, Ohio, and into the Goodyear Tyre and Rubber plant, where more than fifty workers recognized him. But again, no one could remember his name. After that Tarbot dropped out of the news and out of recollection. No one knows what became of him.

6

Hidden Powers

Can a human being vanish "into thin air?" The American broadcaster Long John Nebel has a highly circumstantial account in his book The Way Out World *of how it happened before the eyes of a whole audience, in New York's Paramount Theater.*

During a Thursday afternoon matinée, Nebel's friend William Neff, a well-known conjurer, stepped into a spotlight in front of the curtain and began his patter. As Nebel watched, it seemed to him that he could see light through Neff's body as if he were turning into frosted glass. Slowly, Neff became transparent then disappeared completely, although his voice continued to sound perfectly normal. After a while, a faint outline "like a very fine pencil sketch" began to appear. A few minutes later Neff was back again looking perfectly normal. The audience seems to have assumed that the vanishing was part of his act. As soon as the show was over, Nebel rushed backstage to ask how Neff had done it. Neff seemed surprised, he was not aware that he had "faded." But he admitted that the same thing had happened three years earlier at a theater in Chicago. Moreover, it had happened only a few evenings before as he sat watching television with his wife

Evelyn. He had been alerted to the fact that something was wrong when his wife screamed. When Neff went over and touched her, she screamed again and said, "Who's touching me?" He then hastened from the room to get her a glass of water, and when he returned, she flung her arms around him and said, "I was so frightened – I couldn't see you for a few minutes." Evelyn was so upset that Neff forbade Nebel to question her about it. Nebel can offer no explanation in his book.

Fourth Dimension

Around the turn of the twentieth century, there were a number of theorists who thought they knew the answer. After the invention of non-Euclidean geometry by mathematicians like Riemann and Lobachevsky, many scientists became convinced that there must exist a "fourth dimension" at right angles to the other three (length, breadth and height), and that it is merely the limitations of the human mind that prevent us from seeing it. Professor Johann C. F. Zollner of Leipzig University, suspected that this must be the answer to some of the more baffling questions of psychical research – for example, how the mysterious entity called the poltergeist (also known as the banging ghost), can sometimes throw objects *through* solid walls. (His suggestion was that the objects don't go "through", but into the fourth dimension and out again, just as a giant could step over a wall that would be unscalable to a tortoise.) In 1877, Professor Zollner convinced a large number of sceptics with an interesting experiment with a spiritualist "medium" named Henry Slade. While the medium was in a trance, the "spirits" were asked to tie a knot in a circular piece of cord and they obliged by doing so without breaking the cord. Unbelievers suggested that the medium had merely switched cords, but Zollner insisted that his test conditions were too rigorous for that.

A Russian philosopher named P.D. Ouspensky became so fascinated by the fourth dimension that he devoted most of his first book to this subject. And in *Tertium Organum* he tells how a scientist named Johan Van Manen described how one night, as he lay in bed trying to visualize the fourth dimension, "I plainly saw before me a four-dimensional globe and afterwards a four-dimensional cube . . . ." Unless Van Manen was deceiving himself (although he claimed to be able to recall the globe with ease and the cube with some difficulty), then our minds are capable of grasping that extra dimension. Ouspensky argued that the fourth dimension is the key to a proper understanding of the universe. For example, our three-dimensional understanding cannot grasp the idea of the universe having a beginning or an end, but insight into the fourth dimension would probably allow us to. Albert Einstein – who was unknown at this time – later argued that the fourth dimension is actually time and spoke of the universe as being a kind of "finite yet unbounded" space which curves into the fourth dimension like a sphere.

Among all these speculations, Zollner's experiment stands out as a genuine useful insight. For there can be no possible doubt about the real existence of poltergeists – there are literally thousands of recorded examples of these mischievous "spirits" that throw things and make appalling rackets.

Now many of the mysteries in this book have proved to have down-to-earth solutions. But we should not allow this to deceive us into thinking that there are no genuine mysteries in the world. Nebel's story is a case in point. It is possible, of course, that Nebel simply invented the story – although there is no obvious reason why a famous broadcaster should do so. But the most convincing touch about the story is that apparently Neff had no idea that he had somehow become invisible. And that is consistent with dozens of accounts of people who have exercised apparently "paranormal" powers, and been quite unaware of how they did it.

Doppelgänger

One of the best examples is that of Emilie Sagée. Her case is reported by an American psychical researcher, Robert Dale Owen. Emilie had the curious ability to be in two places at once. Born in 1813 in Dijon, she obtained her first job as a teacher at the age of sixteen. But this job, like so many others, lasted only a short time. This was because Emilie would suddenly turn into two people. For example, in a school for aristocratic young ladies at Neuwelcke, near Womar on the Baltic, her pupils were astonished when, as she was writing on the blackboard, Emilie suddenly became two people, standing side by side, both writing with chalk. At the sudden babble of astonishment, Emilie turned round – and became once again a single person.

On another occasion, as Emilie was helping to fix the dress of a certain Mlle Antoinette de Wrangel, the girl looked into the mirror and saw two Emilies – she fainted.

One warm summer day, as Emilie was picking flowers in the garden, the girls asked the teacher if they might do their lessons outside. The teacher went off to consult the headmistress. Suddenly the form of Emilie was seen sitting in the teacher's chair in the schoolroom. Two of the bolder pupils tried to touch her and said that the apparition felt like muslin. One of them even walked through her. Then the image vanished. A friend of Emilie's, Baroness von Guldenstubbe asked her what had happened. She replied that she had looked into the room through the window, seen that the teacher was not there and felt concerned that the class would misbehave. One of the girls had noticed that the "real Emilie" in the garden became pale and looked ill when her double suddenly appeared. Although Emilie was an excellent teacher, this tendency to turn into two people was altogether too disruptive of discipline and she was asked to leave. Eventually, there is reason to believe that she committed suicide by drowning.

The Germans refer to this "second self" as a "doppelgänger," and the Norwegians as "vardoger," or "forerunner." The poet Goethe experienced an example. One day he was walking home after a heavy shower, and was surprised to see a friend named Friedrich walking in front of him wearing his – Goethe's – dressing gown. He arrived home to find Friedrich in front of the fire in his dressing gown. Friedrich had been on his way to visit Goethe when he was caught in the rain. Goethe's housekeeper had given him the master's dressing gown to put on while his own coat dried out. No doubt he was thinking of Goethe as he put on the dressing gown, and somehow managed to make Goethe see an apparently solid image of himself some distance away.

The poet W. B. Yeats had the same kind of experience. He comments in his autobiography, "One afternoon, I was thinking very intently on a certain fellow student for whom I had a message, which I hesitated about writing. In a couple of days I got a letter from a place some hundreds of miles away where the student was. On the afternoon when I had been thinking so intently, I had suddenly appeared there amid a crowd of people in a hotel, and seeming as solid as if in the flesh. My fellow student [had] seen me, but no one else, and had asked me to come again when the people had gone. I had vanished, but had come again in the middle of the night and given him the message. I myself had no knowledge of either apparition."

Apparitions

In the early years of the Society for Psychical Research, lengthy studies were conducted into this curious ability of human beings to apparently "project" their bodies elsewhere. Most of the cases tend to happen when people are on the point of death – some distant relative sees them walk into the room, looking apparently solid and normal – until they vanish into thin air. But the Society also published a gigantic two-volume work called *Phantasms of the Living*, by Gurney, Myers and

Podmore. It contains hundreds of cases of people who, like Yeats, "appeared" to friends in far distant places without even knowing that they had done so. One of the most famous cases occurred in the year before the Society for Psychical Research was founded. A young student named Beard was engaged to a girl, Miss L. S. Verity. "On a certain Sunday evening in November 1881, having been reading of the great power which the human will is capable of exercising, I determined, with the whole force of my being, that I would be present in spirit in the front bedroom on the second floor of a house situated at 22 Hogarth Road, Kensington." He made the effort at 1.00 a.m. At that moment, Miss Verity woke up, and saw her fiancé standing by her bedside. She screamed and woke her eleven-year-old sister, who also saw Beard. At that point Beard vanished.

In the following year, Beard was involved in an even more remarkable experiment. In December 1882, he decided to try and "appear" in the house in Kew to which Miss Verity and her sister had moved. He sat in a fireside chair and tried to fix his mind on the house. Suddenly he became aware that he could not move his limbs – his own theory was that he had fallen into a "mesmeric sleep." And when, some time later, he regained his normal state by an effort of will, he recorded that he had been in a "trance" state from about 9.30 p.m. until 10.00 p.m. At midnight he made another attempt at "transmission." The following evening he went to call at the house in Kew, and discovered that his fiancée's elder sister was also staying with her – he calls her Mrs L. Mrs L told him that she had seen him the previous evening at 9.30 p.m. going from one room to another. At midnight she saw him yet again as he walked into the bedroom, walked to her bed, and took her long hair in his hand. After this, the "apparition" had taken hold of her hand, and looked at the palm, at which Mrs L remarked, "You need not look at the lines, for I have never had any trouble." When Beard had disappeared again, Mrs L woke her sister who was in the same bed and told her what had happened. Mrs L volunteered this information without any questioning from Beard, and when she had told him her story, Beard took from his pocket his own notes made the previous evening, in which he recorded going into a "trance" at 9.30 p.m., and making another effort to "appear" in the bedroom at Kew at midnight. The interesting part of this second experiment is that the "apparition" was solid enough to hold Mrs L's hair and take her hand – presumably under the impression that she was Miss Verity. Beard himself had no recollection of this.

Beard also made this interesting comment about his first experiment, "Besides exercising my power of volition very strongly, I put forth an effort which I cannot find words to describe. I was conscious of a mysterious influence of some sort permeating my body, and had a distinct impression that I was exercising some force with which I had been hitherto unacquainted, but which I can now at certain times set in motion at will." This seems to demonstrate two things – that Beard used not only his conscious will but also some other kind of will – the power of the unconscious mind – and that once he had learned the trick he could sometimes repeat it. In fact he repeated it once more in 1884, when he again appeared to Miss Verity and stroked her hair.

The American novelist, Theodore Dreiser, tells a story of how his friend, the novelist John Cowper Powys, told him as he left his New York apartment, "I'll appear before you, right here, later this evening. You will see me." Later that evening, he looked up from his book and saw Powys standing in the doorway. Dreiser said, "Well, you've kept your word, John. You're here. Come on in and tell me how you did it." At which Powys disappeared. Dreiser phoned Powys at his house on the Hudson and Powys answered the telephone. When Dreiser said he had just seen him, Powys replied, "I told you I'd be there, and you oughtn't to be surprised." But he would never explain to Dreiser how he did it. Obviously, Powys *had* mastered the trick that Beard talks about. And he hints at what lay behind it in a passage in his autobiography in which he says, about the Roman amphitheater in Verona, "Alone in that Roman circle, under those clouds from which no drop of rain fell, the thaumaturgic [i.e. magical] element in my nature rose to such a pitch that I felt, as I have only done once or twice since, that I really *was* endowed with some sort of supernatural power . . . ." What Powys is saying is that this ability is *natural*, but that we only become aware of it under certain unusual circumstances.

Belief in such powers is not a part of our western tradition of thinking. But in the east, they are much more taken for granted. There is an interesting example in a book called *Autobiography of a Yogi* by Paramhansa Yogananda (1951), a famous Hindu guru, who became well known in America in the 1940s. W. Y. Evans-Wentz, who writes the introduction, has no doubt of its genuineness. In the second chapter, Yogananda describes how, at the age of twelve, he went to Benares to see a Yogi called Swami Pranabananda. His father has asked him to make contact with a friend called Babu,

Theodore Dreiser

whose address he had lost. Yogananda found the Swami, a rather stout man, sitting cross-legged on the floor, wearing only a loin cloth. Although he had never seen him before, the Swami instantly recognized him. He then went on to say, "Of course I will locate Babu for you" – before the boy had mentioned why he was there. After a short time, the Swami went into meditation, and Yogananda began to feel nervous and unsure, wondering when he was going to meet Babu. At this point, reading his mind, the Swami said, "Don't get worried. The man you wish to see will be with you in half an hour." Half an hour later, someone came up the stairs. The boy went out to find Babu about to enter the room. He asked him how he came to be there. Babu replied, "Everything is mysterious today! Less than an hour ago I had just finished my bath in the Ganges when Swami Pranabananda approached me. I have no idea how he knew I was there at that time. He said, 'Bhagabati's son is waiting for you in my apartment. Will you come with me?' I gladly agreed. As we proceeded hand in hand, the Swami in his wooden sandals was strangely able to outpace me, though I wore these stout walking shoes.

"'How long will it take you to reach my place?' the Swami asked.

"'About half an hour.'

"'I have something else to do at present.' The Swami gave me an enigmatical glance. 'I must leave you behind. You can join me in my house, where Bhagabati's son and I will be awaiting you.'

"Before I could remonstrate, he dashed swiftly past me and disappeared in the crowd. I walked here as fast as possible."

Yogananda said, "I cannot believe my ears! Am I losing my mind? Did you meet him in a vision, or did you actually see him, touch his hand, and hear the sound of his feet?"

"I don't know what you're driving at!" He flushed angrily. "I am not lying to you. Can't you understand that only through the Swami could I have known that you were waiting at this place for me?"

"Why, that man, Swami Pranabanda, has not left my sight a moment since I first came here about an hour ago." I blurted out the whole story.

His eyes opened widely. "Are we living in this material age, or are we dreaming? I never expected to witness such a miracle in my life! I thought this Swami was just an ordinary man, and now I find he can materialise an extra body and work through it!"

The chapter in Yogananda's book is entitled, "The Saint With Two Bodies."

But later in the book, Yogananda tells an even more remarkable story. Yogananda's own special guru, Sri Yukteswar, had died on March 9, 1936. But he had promised his disciple to return. On June 12, 1936, Yogananda was sitting in his bedroom in the Regent Hotel in Bombay when he suddenly experienced a vision of the Lord Krishna. The room seemed to fill with light, and when it vanished a moment later, Yogananda felt that it was a sign that some remarkable event was going to occur. One week later, on June 19, 1936, Yogananda was roused from his meditation by a beatific light. Standing in front of him was his master, Sri Yukteswar. Yogananda was so overwhelmed that he threw his arms around him, and had no doubt whatever that he was real. He asked Yukteswar whether he was "wearing" his own physical body. Yukteswar replied, "Yes, my child, I am the same. This is a flesh and blood body. Though I see it as ethereal, to your sight it is physical. From the cosmic atoms I created an entirely new body, exactly like that cosmic-dream physical body which you laid beneath the dream-sands at Puri in your dream world. I am in truth resurrected – not on earth but on an astral planet." Yogananda goes on to describe a long conversation with his guru which must have continued for several hours before Yukteswar took his leave, and vanished.

According to the history books, Marshal Ney – one of Napoleon's greatest commanders – died before a firing squad on December 7, 1815, in the Luxembourg Gardens in Paris. But there is interesting evidence to suggest that Ney did not die, but simply vanished into oblivion.

Michel Ney was born in 1769 and rose through army ranks, finally becoming one of Napoleon's most trusted generals. But when Napoleon's victorious enemies entered Paris on March 31, 1814, Napoleon abdicated and was sent to Elba. Ney swore allegiance to the Bourbon king Louis XVIII.

When Napoleon escaped from Elba and returned to France, Ney could not find it in his heart to arrest his old commander – instead he joined him. It was Ney who led the last great charge at the Battle of Waterloo. After that, Napoleon went into his final exile at St Helena, and Ney was sentenced to death for treason.

Even the Duke of Wellington intervened to try and save him, but the king refused to relent. He even decreed that the Marshal should be executed by some of his old comrades. Many of the firing squad were weeping when Ney shouted, "Straight to the heart! Fire!"

An official report declared that Ney had been killed by "twelve balls, nine in the breast, three in the head."

Three weeks later, an ex-soldier named Philip Petrie (who had deserted from the army and become a sailor) approached a passenger on a ship sailing from Bordeaux to Charleston, South Carolina and asked, "Aren't you Marshal Ney?" The passenger shook his head. "Marshal Ney was executed two weeks ago in Paris." Petrie was to tell this story shortly before his death in 1874. Oddly enough, the passenger who looked like Marshal Ney was sailing under the name of Peter Stewart Ney.

In 1819, Peter Ney became a schoolmaster in Mocksville, North Carolina. But when Napoleon died in 1821, Peter Ney fainted at the sight of the newspaper carrying the story and subsequently attempted suicide by cutting his throat – fortunately the knife broke. He later told the father of a pupil, "With the death of Napoleon, my last hope is gone." It seemed that he was still hoping that Napoleon would return to power and that he could return to France.

On his deathbed in 1846, Peter Ney declared that he was, indeed, Napoleon's marshal. The men of the firing squad had been given instructions to wait until he gave the order "fire!," and fell down. To anyone watching, it would have seemed that he was shot. In fact, according to Ney, the bullets passed over his head.

When Louis Napoleon came to the throne of France in 1848, he ordered that monuments should replace all the graves of Napoleon's generals. But oddly enough, Ney's widow refused this honour. There is one more piece of evidence. In the records of the hospital to which Ney's body was taken, it is recorded that the body was unmarked by bullets.

Our natural tendency is to regard all this as pure invention. Yet a moment's thought will show that there is nothing here that contradicts what has been said above. And if we can accept the evidence of *Phantasms of the Living*, in which there are dozens of cases of people who have appeared to relatives at the moment of death, and even after it, then there also seems to be sound reason for believing that part of us survives physical death.

The novelist Wilbur Wright has advanced the interesting theory that, at the point of death, some of those unusual powers mentioned by Powys are released in most of us, which explains the "apparitions" seen by relatives of the dying. It could be compared to the sensation described by so many people on the point of drowning, of having their whole life flash in front of their eyes in a split second. In other words, there seems to be strong evidence that human beings possess powers of which they are normally unaware, but which can be contacted in moments of emergency or excitement.

What is it that prevents us from making use of these powers? The answer clearly is – habit. Our minds tend to be confined to everyday limitations, and to the triviality of every day living. So we never make the slightest effort to call upon "hidden powers." Moreover, there is something in everyday life itself that actively impedes this kind of insight. In *Modes of Thought*, the philosopher Alfred North Whitehead makes the interesting observation that language itself, with its dictionary definition of words and its neat full stops at the end of every sentence, gives us a quite false sensation that the world around us can also be reduced to a neat pattern. This sensation gives us a deep feeling of comfort. Scientists, in particular, like this feeling that the world can be totally explained, and that by conducting experiments in laboratories we shall one day know everything there is to know. Modern cosmologists firmly believe that they are on the point of discovering a "theory of everything", which will explain the whole universe.

There is a fundamental fallacy here. We can see it if we think about the problem of where space ends or when time began. It is quite obvious that the theory of the "Big Bang" begs the whole question. It may tell us when and how the universe began (although even that is doubtful), but it still leaves us with the same basic question of where it came from and what there was before. It is like the Hindu myth that the world is held up on the back of an elephant, which in turn is held up on a camel which in turn . . . . We can see that this myth is based upon a simple failure to understand about gravity and the fact that objects in outer space do not need to be held up by other objects. The recognition that objects in empty space do *not* begin to fall is a completely new way of seeing things.

Human beings are not only unwilling to consider a new way of seeing things, they are actively resentful at the very idea. This is the reason that various well known scientists – the latest is Carl Sagan – have written books denouncing what they regard as superstitions. They are not entirely wrong. A scientist who doubted that David Lang *had* actually disappeared as he was crossing a field would be perfectly correct. The whole story was an invention.

But it would be a mistake to leap from this recognition to the notion that the world is a perfectly solid, rational place in which unexplainable things never take place.

In the nineteenth century, a series of strange poltergeist events in the house of the Fox family in New York State led to the foundation of what became known as Spiritualism. Serious thinkers were sufficiently intrigued to found the Society for Psychical Research, to try to place these strange anomalies on a scientific basis. But although most reasonable people will concede that they proved the existence of "strange phenomena" beyond all possible doubt, they completely failed in their attempt to draw such problems as life after death into the realm of science. In our own time, the phenomenon of UFOs has posed the same problem. At first regarded as proof – by the believers – of visitors from outer space, it has become increasingly clear that the whole phenomenon simply refuses to be fitted into any sensible scientific category. And while the climate of opinion is changing, so an increasing number of people – including scientists – are coming to accept the reality of UFO phenomena, it is also becoming clear that the "aliens" do not seem to share the same limitations as human beings. In fact, they seem to behave very much like the "spirits" of the nineteenth century.

All this raises an interesting question. Is it possible that the "aliens" are beings like ourselves – but beings who have learned to control those "supernatural powers" that John Cowper Powys felt as he stood in the amphitheater in Verona? To consider this possibility is not, as sceptics like to assure us, to be on the verge of joining the lunatic fringe and losing the power of reason. It is merely to recognize that what we call "normality" may be no more than a prejudice which is about to be abolished.

Index